# SOUTHERN BAPTISTS
## and the
# DOCTRINE
## of
# ELECTION

Robert B. Selph, Pastor

Miller Valley Baptist Church

Prescott, Arizona

Sprinkl
Harriso

D1430661

For a book list, write to:
Sprinkle Publications
P. O.  Box 1094
Harrisonburg, VA   22801

## ACKNOWLEDGEMENTS
## and THANKS

To Ernest C. Reisinger, for the encouragement and vision he has given to labor for the good of God's work within the Southern Baptist Convention.

To Dr. Tom Nettles, whose research is used extensively in this book. His contribution to Southern Baptists will never be measured in this life.

To Walt Chantry, Richard Moore, Albert Wycoff, and DeWayne Adams, for their assistance with this book.

To the den Dulk Foundation, for financial assistance.

To Ed and Cindy Tischler, for their computer.

To my wonderful wife, Cathi. God alone knows how she has encouraged and supported me on the way to the Celestial City. She also typed this book.

To my children, the sweetest kids in the world.

To the Miller Valley Baptist Church—the faithful brethren who stand with me, bear with me, and constantly uplift me.

# TABLE OF CONTENTS

*For of Him, and through Him, and to Him, are all things: to whom be glory forever. Amen.*

*Romans 11:36*

*Blessed be the God and Father of our Lord Jesus Christ, who hath blessed us with all spiritual blessings in heavenly places in Christ: According as He hath chosen us in Him before the foundation of the world, that we should be holy and without blame before Him in love: having predestinated us unto the adoption of children by Jesus Christ to Himself, according to the good pleasure of His will, to the praise of the glory of His grace, wherein He hath made us accepted in the Beloved.*

*Ephesians 1:3-6*

*That in the ages to come He might show the exceeding riches of His grace in His kindness toward us through Christ Jesus.*

*Ephesians 2:7*

# Unconditional Election –A Southern Baptist Heritage

The Southern Baptist Convention has been blessed and mightily used of God. Through the years Baptists have been rightly called "people of the Book" due to their unswerving conviction that the Bible is the Word of God. Baptists have had a tenacious grip upon the Bible as their only rule of faith and practice. The priority of their cooperative effort in obeying Christ in the Great Commission has driven them worldwide with the Good News of the Gospel. The watchword for this people is evangelism. They have maintained this commitment to missions and evangelism when other denominations have dropped the ball and traded the preaching of soul-saving truth for a gospel of social reform.

However, there is a doctrinal heritage to the Southern Baptist Convention that many Baptists are not aware of. The central truth of this doctrinal heritage, which has been "decentralized" over the years, is the doctrine of Unconditional Election. This teaching was not merely a side issue which provided seminary students with some nonessential moments of trivial debate. This truth of Unconditional Election was the foundation, the heart, and the hub of all Bible truth. This doctrine was for Baptists the backbone of Gospel preaching and missionary endeavor. The worship, evangelism, and service of Southern

7

# UNCONDITIONAL ELECTION

Baptists for eighty years was molded and directed by this precious truth. Hymns, confessions, catechisms, and doctrinal standards signed by seminary professors all reflected the universal acknowledgment of this doctrine among Baptists.

Today many Southern Baptists, along with most evangelicals, consider the doctrine of Election to be nonessential, detrimental to evangelism, a threat to missionary zeal, a contradiction to the love and fairness of God, and divisive to the churches. This attitude is so different from what Baptists used to embrace. For example, consider this statement by J. B. Gambrell. Brother Gambrell was president of the Southern Baptist Convention (1917-1920), one-time editor of the Baptist Standard, professor of ecclesiology at Southern Baptist Theological Seminary, editor of the Baptist Record in Mississippi and generally prominent Southern Baptist in the first part of the 20th century. He wrote a book entitled <u>Baptist Principles Reset</u>, in which he spoke of the obligation of Baptists to teach their principles. After talking about "milk-sop, clap-trap evangelism," he inserts this:

> "We may invigorate our faith and renew our courage by reflecting that divine power has always attended the preaching of doctrine when done in the true spirit of preaching. Great revivals have accompanied the heroic preaching of the doctrines of grace—predestination, election, and that whole lofty mountain range of doctrines upon which Jehovah sits enthroned, sovereign in grace, as in all things else. God honors the preaching that honors Him. There is entirely too much milk-sop preaching nowadays—trying to cajole sinners to enter upon a truce with their Maker —'Quit sinning and join the church.' The situation does not call for a truce, but for a surrender. Let us bring on the heavy

8

artillery of heaven and thunder away at the stuck-up age as Whitefield, Edwards, Spurgeon, and Paul did and there will be many slain of the Lord raised up to walk in newness of life."[1]

Brother Gambrell obviously felt the preaching of Election was central to a God-honoring, life-changing Gospel. Why did he feel that way?

One might object, asking, "What did Gambrell mean by 'Election'?" Did he mean "Unconditional Election" was involved in true Gospel preaching, or could he have meant an Arminian election which is conditioned upon man's free will? Gambrell answered this question for us in the above quotation by his doctrinal identification with several men: Whitefield, Edwards, Spurgeon, and Paul. There is no doubt historically what Gambrell meant by Election and Predestination. It was a Gospel of God's indisputable and absolute sovereignty. This was the Gospel of our Southern Baptist forefathers for the first eighty years of the Southern Baptist Convention.

I would like to present a clear definition of the doctrine of Unconditional Election as stated by J. P. Boyce, founder and first president of Southern Seminary in Louisville, and president of the Southern Baptist Convention (1872-1879, 1888). His definition of Unconditional Election is found in his Abstract of Systematic Theology and is taken from his sermon by that title.

"The theory of Calvinists as to election is that God (not man) of His own purpose (in accordance with His will, and not from any obligation to men, nor because of any will of man), has from eternity (the period of God's action, not in time in which man acts), determined to save (not has actually saved, but simply determined so to do, and to save, not merely to confer gospel or church

9

# UNCONDITIONAL ELECTION

privileges upon) <u>a definite number of mankind</u> (not the whole race, nor indefinitely, merely some of them, nor indefinitely a certain proportionate part, but a definite number), <u>as individuals</u> (not the whole or part of the race, nor of a nation, nor of a church, nor of a class, as of believers or the pious; but individuals) <u>not for or because of any merit or work of theirs, nor of any value to him of them</u> (not for their good works, or their holiness or excellence, or their faith, or their spiritual sanctification although the choice is to a salvation attained through faith and sanctification; nor for their value to him, though their salvation tends greatly to the manifested glory of his grace); <u>but of good pleasure simply because he was pleased so to choose</u>."[2]

Boyce used the following scripture verses in support of his position:

| | |
|---|---|
| Ephesians 1:4-6, 11 | Matthew 11:25,26 |
| II Thessalonians 2:13 | I Corinthians 1:26 30 |
| Acts 13:48 | II Timothy 1:9 |
| Romans 8:28-30, 33; | Revelation 13:8; 17:8 |
| 9:11-24 | Ephesians 2:1-3 |
| John 1:13, 3:3-8; 5:21; | James 1:18 |
| 6:37-65; 15:16; 17:2 | |

This definition is clear. Dr. Boyce believed and taught Unconditional Election. This Election to salvation was not based upon God looking into the future, seeing which men would choose Him, and then electing those men unto salvation. Rather, our Baptist fathers preached the God of absolute and indisputable sovereignty who chose His elect with nothing moving Him with respect to whom He chose, except His own good pleasure and distinguishing mercy. This is <u>not</u> to say they were "hyper-Calvinists" who did not believe men were saved by faith. They did preach the Gospel duties of repentance and faith, and they did so powerfully in a worldwide missionary effort. But they preached these duties in the context of a sovereign God who has "mercy upon whom He will have mercy . . ." Their God was exalted in sovereignty with men humbled at His feet.

In the following chapter, testimonies are provided about Professor Boyce's influence in the seminary. He counted the doctrine of Unconditional Election so important that he sought to bring all of his students to embrace it. It was also said that Dr. Boyce taught the students how to sympathize with lost souls and to have a warm zeal in the work of the Gospel. Contrary to human logic or popular opinion, the truth of election and the duty of evangelism flow and work together beautifully (see chapter four.)

Another brief definition of Unconditional Election can be found in the <u>Abstract of Principles</u>.

> V. Election - "Election is God's eternal choice of some persons unto everlasting life–not because of foreseen merit in them, but of his mere mercy in Christ–in consequence of which choice they are called, justified and glorified." [3]

The following is an excerpt from the Fundamental Laws of the Southern Baptist Theological Seminary written into its charter on April 30, 1858:

> "Every Professor of the institution shall be a member of a regular Baptist Church; and all persons accepting Professorships in this Seminary, shall be considered by such acceptance, as engaging to teach in accordance with, and not contrary to, the <u>Abstract of Principles</u>

hereinafter laid down." [4]

Every professor in the first seminary promised–and still does today–to teach Unconditional Election, which the Abstract of Principles qualified as "not because of foreseen merit in them." Election has nothing to do with man's goodness or foreseen faith–only God's sovereign purpose.

The Charleston Baptist Association, the first Baptist association in the South, was founded in 1751. This association had the first Southern Baptist church in its membership, and its doctrinal statement was the <u>Second London Baptist Confession of 1689.</u> These truths were believed and preached by our forefathers until the early 1900s. The following statement is taken from the 1689 Confession concerning "Election." More of this confession is given in the next chapter within the section on W. B. Johnson.

3. By the decree of God, for the manifestation of his glory, some men and angels are predestinated, or foreordained to eternal life through Jesus Christ,[a] to the praise of his glorious grace;[b] others being left to act in their sin to their just condemnation, to the praise of his glorious justice.[c]

a. I Tim. 5:21; Matt. 25:34. b. Eph. 1:5, 6. c. Rom. 9:22, 23; Jude 4.

4. These angels and men thus predestinated and foreordained, are particularly and unchangeably designed, and their number so certain and definite, that it cannot be either increased or diminished.[d]

d. 2 Tim. 2:19; John 13:8.

5. Those of mankind that are predestined to life,

God, before the foundation of the world was laid, according to his eternal and immutable purpose, and the secret counsel and good pleasure of his will, hath chosen in Christ unto everlasting glory, out of his mere free grace and love,[e] without any other thing in the creature as a condition or cause moving him thereunto.[f]

e. Eph. 1:4, 9, 11;  Rom. 8:30;  II Tim. 1:9;  I Thess. 5:9.  f. Rom. 9:13, 16;  Eph. 2:5, 12.

Another look at J. B. Gambrell's statement might carry a bit more significance now with our terms defined.

"We may invigorate our faith and renew our courage by reflecting that divine power has always attended the preaching of doctrine when done in the true spirit of preaching. Great revivals have accompanied the heroic preaching of the doctrines of grace—predestination, election, and that whole lofty mountain range of doctrines upon which Jehovah sits enthroned, sovereign in grace, as in all things else.  God honors the preaching that honors Him.  There is entirely too much milk-sop preaching nowadays—trying to cajole sinners to enter upon a truce with their Maker—'Quit sinning and join the church.'  The situation does not call for a truce, but for a surrender. Let us bring on the heavy artillery of heaven and thunder away at the stuck-up age as Whitefield, Edwards, Spurgeon and Paul did and there will be many slain of the Lord raised up to walk in newness of life."

I believe Brother Gambrell makes several points that should be considered in light of the present methods of evangelism prevalent among evangelicals today.  First, he states that true evangelistic preaching consists of the preaching of doctrine, specifically the doctrines of grace. To Gambrell, there was no distinction between preaching doctrine and preaching Jesus. The pulpits were serious in the teaching of God's entire Word with the conviction that God's truth alone could enlighten the mind, crush the conscience, and subdue the heart. Jesus was the center of every doctrine and every doctrine exalted Jesus. The doctrines of grace, as Gambrell said, were the foundational doctrines that brought honor to God and to His Son such as no other doctrines could do. When they preached God's electing and sovereign grace they were, in fact, preaching the purest Jesus. Today the fear of "turning people off" with having to "think" through doctrinal truths has led the pulpits overall to a shallowness that has dulled the cutting edge of soul-saving truth.

Secondly, Gambrell believed greater emphasis in preaching should be given to the exalting of God. Jehovah is to be set before the eyes of sinners in His incomparable glory and in His awful majesty. Sinners need to tremble before the infinite Judge of heaven and earth. He is to be enthroned. He is sovereign. He was, is, and is to come in full display of indisputable rule over all. Gambrell knew that only the doctrine of Unconditional Election accomplishes such exaltation of Jehovah.

Thirdly, Gambrell spoke of a simplistic, man-centered evangelism, such as, "Just sell folks on a limited number of half-truths in order to get their "decision" and church membership and hope they stick enough to grow in that decision." Apparently in Gambrell's day the Gospel presentation had been watered down to pursuing a human decision for Jesus and an external commitment to a church. Today we may not want to admit to our evangelism being described in such a way. However, the church is also frustrated in trying to get its converts to follow through as true disciples. In our "decision-oriented" meetings man has become the sovereign one who is pleaded with to give God a chance. What a difference between our converts who "consent" for God to save them by "accepting Jesus" and the New Testament converts who pleaded in desperation for God in Christ to have mercy upon their poor, miserable souls.

Fourthly, Gambrell saw the correlation between preaching Election as it is seen in the whole of God's saving truths, and the duty of repentance. The doctrine of Election exalted God as God, His Word as final and His Law as holy and binding. The God of sovereign majesty would hold no parleys with fallen man but demanded a full-scale surrender of heart and life. There was no taking Jesus as Savior without bowing obediently before Him as Lord. Man was made to fear the living God and to hope only in His sovereign mercy. Gambrell spoke of a dynamic transformation of heart—a newness of life—which the great doctrines of Gospel grace alone bring about. Again, what a difference between our thinking today and that of early Baptists. They did not have to devise elaborate "follow-up" programs to keep supposed converts from falling by the wayside. They did their follow-up work prior to conversion so that conversion meant a radical and continuous change of life.

Lastly, Gambrell spoke of how the great doctrines of Election and Predestination are positive encouragements—motivation and inspiration to the work of Gospel preaching. He, in fact, said that if you want to be really invigorated in your faith and renewed in your courage to the task of evangelism, reflect upon how God has used the preaching of the historic doctrines of grace (Election, Predestination, etc.) to bring many to Himself in salvation. This is far from what many say about the detrimental effect Election would have on evangelism and missions.

15

# UNCONDITIONAL ELECTION

It was the assurance of Unconditional Election that brought the Apostle Paul such tenacity and drive in his Gospel labors. He told Timothy, "Therefore I endure all things for the sake of the elect, that they also may obtain the salvation which is in Christ Jesus with eternal glory" (II Timothy 2:10). Paul knew he would not fail. He was deeply convinced that his Gospel preaching and imprisonments were not in vain. He could stand beside river-banks, inside synagogues, before kings, or lay bound in dark dungeons and preach the unsearchable riches of Christ, fully persuaded that every one of those chosen before the world was formed would eventually bow before the preached Christ for salvation. The word preached would not return void. It would accomplish exactly what God sent it out to do. It is God who prospers His word with success—not man (Isaiah 55:11). His sovereign purpose determines when hearts will be broken or hardened.

This is the confidence that supported the modern mission-ary movement—"God will save His people from their sins—we shall not fail!" We do not have to cut corners or shave off the rough edges of the Gospel. We must preach the sovereignty and holiness of God, the utter pollution and guilt of the human soul, the absolute necessity of personal repentance—all the truths that make the natural man to quiver with disgust and boil with rage— and then rejoice with assurance that though men walk away, yet God is honored and some will respond! To the amazement of mortal man, the truths God uses to effect the greater success of true conversions are the truths that most exalt God, most debase man, and most magnify Jehovah's grace. Christ must be declared boldly—fervently—widely, and all of His sheep will hear His voice and follow Him. He will not lose one of them (John 6:37-39; 10:27).

# SOUTHERN BAPTIST HERITAGE

As the reader considers statements of our Baptist fathers in the following chapter, let these questions be asked and pondered. Did these historical men of God see Unconditional Election as a threat to evangelism? Were any of these men stifled in their participation in worldwide missionary endeavors? Did they project the Almighty as being unfair or partial? Did they see men as mere robots or puppets without responsibility? Did they believe in Unconditional Election but feel that it should not be publicly proclaimed? Was their ability to present the free offer of the Gospel to every creature in this earth reduced to hapless insincerity? Is there any evidence of the doctrine of Election making their churches dead and cold? Did they incorporate this doctrine into their Gospel presentation, or was it reserved only for classroom discussions in theological institutions?

Many have been the objections against this doctrine, but I would ask the reader to give these men a fair hearing, regardless of how you have been warned about this doctrine in the past. I am quite confident that an open-minded inquiry will produce the same conclusion to which I have come—the doctrine of Unconditional Election is the foundational doctrinal heritage of the Southern Baptist Convention and of Baptists in general.

Following Chapter 2, the next two chapters are devoted to answering the inevitable questions that are raised by sincere people about the doctrine of Election, and to looking at the relevancy of this doctrine to our faith and ministries today.

### Saints Beloved in Christ.
Eph. 1:3

1. *Jesus, we bless thy Father's name;*
   *Thy God and ours is one, the same;*
   *What heavenly blessings, from his throne,*
   *Flow down to sinners through his Son!*

2. *"Christ be my first Elect," he said;*
   *Then chose our souls in Christ our Head;*
   *Before he gave the mountains birth,*
   *Or laid foundations for the earth.*

3. *Thus did eternal love begin*
   *To raise us up from death and sin;*
   *Our characters were then decreed,*
   *Blameless in love, a holy seed.*

4. *Predestinated to be sons,*
   *Born by degrees, but chose at once;*
   *A new regenerated race,*
   *To praise the glory of his grace.*

5. *With Christ, our Lord, we share a part*
   *In the affections of his heart;*
   *Nor shall our souls be thence removed,*
   *Till he forgets his First Beloved.*

*HYMN TUNE: Canonbury*

*Sample hymn from the days of our SBC forefathers*[88]

# Significant Baptist Voices in History

This chapter is devoted to our forefathers in the faith. We do not worship their opinions nor reverence their statements as inspired scripture. We profit from their wisdom to keep our own conclusions and interpretations in check lest we fall for some "new wind of doctrine." As we consider their statements we readily see how Baptists, yea much of Christ's church, has changed. These quotes are given to show that Unconditional Election is not new nor is it "off the wall." Only brief samples are given from the wealth of Baptist History that is available. Also quoted are John Newton, Jonathan Edwards, George Whitefield, and Matthew Henry, because of the way God so richly poured out His Spirit upon their labors. From earlier Baptists to Southern Baptists, their voices blend still to exalt God as Sovereign Lord who will save His elect, not by their merit or foreseen faith, but by His free grace.

**Roger Williams** (1603-1684) was the first Baptist to establish a Baptist church in America, and was a strong Calvinist. He founded his defense of religious liberty upon Calvinistic theology. He stated, "Since only God can give faith, it does not lie within the power of the magistrate to command a man to believe or worship in any particular way. The allowance of error in civil society does not harm the church, for not one elect of God shall perish." [5]

In addressing the futility of forced worship by civil authorities, Williams states,

"Accordingly, an unbelieving soul, being dead in sin, although he be changed from one worship to another, like a dead man shifted into several changes of apparel cannot please God. And consequently, whatever such an unbelieving and unregenerate person acts in worship of religion, it is sin."

"So here, whatever be the soul infection breathed out from the lying lips of a plague sick Pharisee, yet not one elect or chosen of God shall perish. God's sheep are safe in his eternal hand and counsel and he that knows his material knows also his mystical stars their numbers and calls them everyone by name. None falls into the ditch on the blind Pharisees' back but such as were ordained to that condemnation, both guide and followers."

"Me thinks I discern a three-fold guilt upon such civil powers as imposed upon and enforce the conscience. Either to depart from that worship which is persuaded of, or to exercise any worship which it has not faith in. First, of an appearance of that Arminian popish doctrine of free-will as if it lay in their own power and ability to believe upon the magistrate's command. Since it is confessed that what is submitted to by any without faith is sin be it never so true and holy. Second, since God only opens the heart and works the will, it seems to be a high presumption to suppose that together with a command restraining from or constraining to worship, that God is also to be forced or commanded to give faith to open the heart and to incline the will. And third, a guilt of a hypocrisy of their subjects and people enforcing them to act and practice in matters of religion and worship against the doubts and checks of their consciences. Causing, their bodies to worship when their souls are far off, to draw near with their lips, their hearts being far off." [6]

**Obadiah Holmes** (1607-1682) was a staunch leader and pastor among America's earliest Baptists. Contemporary with Williams and Clarke, Holmes really exemplifies more than any other the stance of these early Baptists. He, too, was heavily persecuted then for his position on "soul liberty."

The following is found in Gaustad's book entitled, The Last Will and Testimony of Obadiah Holmes: "Understandably, Holmes' confession of faith makes many of the same points enunciated in the confessions of other early Baptists, both in America and abroad. The influential London Confession of 1644, signed by William Kiffin and John Spilsbury among others, spells out some fifty-three articles of faith in about four times the length which Holmes uses for his thirty-five points.

"That faith stands unmistakably in the Calvinist tradition, as did that of the London churches, the Boston church, and the whole surrounding and dominating Puritan culture. As in Puritan theology, Holmes' Calvinism was expressed through the vehicle of a covenant of grace that displaced and made forever obsolete the old covenant of works which God had made with Adam. Holmes states, 'Those destined to be saved are, to be sure, those whom God chooses to save, His elect, 'for He knows who are His . . .,' and because man does not save himself, he cannot cause himself to be lost. All that are in the covenant of grace 'shall never fall away or perish.' The saints persevere because God does not weaken or change. Those who come to Him He will in no way and at no time cast out. Calvinist Baptists in London (William Kiffin among them) endorsed the small pamphlet published by Boston's pastor, John Russell, in 1680 (A Brief Narrative . . .), saying that the Boston Baptists 'have declared their perfect agreement with us both in matters of faith and worship, as set down in our late confession. And a later Newport pastor provided an abstract of 'a small book written by John Clarke . . . containing his judgment and the judgment of the Church respecting that soul-supporting doctrine of personal election . . .' The Calvinist character of these New England Baptists in the seventeenth century is thus apparent, and the testimony of Obadiah Holmes places him centrally in that tradition." [7]

**Benjamin Keach** became pastor of the Baptist Church in Horsleydown, London in 1668. He was instrumental in forming the second London Confession of 1689 which is eminently strong in the doctrines of election. Keach comments on Matthew 20:16–"Election is an act of God's sovereignty or the good pleasure of His will for which He passed by the fallen angels and only sets His heart upon and chooses some of the lost sons of Adam. Election necessarily presupposeth some chosen and the rest passed by." Again he states, "Election to everlasting life is an absolute act of God's sovereign grace without any respect had to our foreseen faith or holiness or obedience because election is the cause of our faith and holiness and not faith and holiness the cause of election." [8]

**John Bunyan** (1628-1688) was a Baptist preacher in England

and author of the famous <u>Pilgrim's Progress</u>. He also produced a tract entitled <u>Reprobation Asserted</u>, which was published in 1674. In this tract Bunyan states, "Now as touching the elect, they are by this decree confined to that limited number of persons that must amount to the complete making up of the fulness of the mystical body of Christ, yea so confined by this eternal purpose that nothing can be diminished from or added thereunto . . ." Further along he says, "Were the elect left to themselves, they, through the wickedness of their heart, would perish as do others. Neither could all the reasonable persuasive prevalent arguments of the Gospel of God in Christ prevail to make any receive it and live . . . so there is also the grace of election; which grace kindly overruleth and winneth the spirit of the chosen . . . There is a remnant that receive this grace; they being appointed, I say, thereto, before the world began; preserved in time from that which would undo them, and enabled to embrace the glorious gospel of grace, and peace, and life." [9]

<u>**Matthew Henry**</u> (1662-1714) wrote the widely-used commentary bearing his name. Commenting on Romans 8:29,30, Henry says, "Whom He did foreknow He also did predestinate to be conformed to the image of His Son. All that God designed for glory and happiness as the end He decreed to grace and holiness as the way. Not, whom He did foreknow to be holy those He predestinated to be so. The counsels and decrees of God do not truckle to the frail and fickle will of men; no, God's foreknowledge of the saints is the same with the everlasting love wherewith He is said to have loved them, Jeremiah 31:3. God's knowing His people is the same with His owning them, Psalm 1:6; John 10:14; II Timothy 2:19. Words of knowledge often in scripture denote affection; so here: Elect according to the

foreknowledge of God, I Peter 1:2. And the same word is rendered fore-ordained, I Peter 1:20. Whom He did foreknow, that is, whom He designed for his friends and favourites. 'I know thee by name,' said God to Moses, Exodus 33:12. Whom He did predestinate, those He also called, not only with the external call (so many are called that were not chosen, Matthew 20:16; 22:14), but with the internal and effectual call. The former comes to the ear only, but this to the heart. All that God did from eternity predestinate to grace and glory He does in the fulness of time, effectually call. The call is then effectual when we come at the call; and we then come at the call when the Spirit draws us, convinces the conscience of guilt and wrath, enlightens the understanding, bows the will, persuades and enables us to embrace Christ in the promises, makes us willing in the day of His power."

Also commenting on Romans 11:6,7, he states, "This is called a remnant according to the election of grace; they are such as were chosen from eternity in the counsels of divine love to be vessels of grace and glory. Whom He did predestinate those He called. If the difference between them and others He made purely by the grace of God, as certainly it is (I have reserved them, saith He, to myself), then it must needs be according to the election; for we are sure that whatever God does He does it according to the counsel of His own will. Now concerning this remnant, we may observe, first, whence it takes rise, from the free grace of God (v. 6), that grace which excludes works. The eternal election, in which the difference between some and others is first founded, is purely of grace, free grace; not for the sake of works done or foreseen; if so, it would not be grace. Gratia non est ullo modo gratia, si non sit omni modo gratuita— it is not grace, properly so called, if it be not perfectly free.

Election is purely according to the good pleasure of His will, Ephesians 1:5. The rest were blinded, v. 7. Some are chosen and called, and the call is made effectual. But others are left to perish in their unbelief. [10]

**Jonathan Edwards**, (1703-1758) the renowned American theologian and preacher during the Great Awakening of 1734-1744 stated; "And whereas it has been said, that the Calvinistic doctrine of necessity saps the foundations of all reigns and virtue, and tends to the greatest licentiousness of practice: this objection is built on the pretence, that our doctrine renders vain all means and endeavours, in order to be virtuous and religious. Which pretence has been already particularly considered in the fifth Section of this Part; where it has been demonstrated, that this doctrine has no such tendency; but that as the notion of contingence, which their doctrine implies in the certain consequences, overthrows all connexion in every degree, between endeavour and event, means and end."

Edwards also stated, "And as it has been now shown, how the doctrine of determining efficacious grace certainly follows from things proved in the foregoing discourse; hence will necessarily follow the doctrine of particular, eternal, absolute election. For if men are made true saints, no otherwise than as God makes them so, and distinguishes them from others, by His efficacious power and influence, that decides and fixes the event; and God thus makes some saints, and not others, on design or purpose, and (as has been now observed) no designs of God are new; it follows, that God thus distinguished from others, all that ever become true saints, by His eternal design or decree. I might also show, how God's certain foreknowledge must suppose an absolute decree, and how such a decree can be proved to a demonstration from it: but that this discourse may not be lengthened out too much, that must be omitted for the present." [11]

**George Whitefield** (1714-1770) was an English preacher and revivalist. By common consent he was the greatest preacher of the 18th century and of his preaching gifts J. C. Ryle wrote, "No Englishman, I believe, dead or alive, has equaled him." Whitefield was at the center of the Great Awakening, reaching many with the Gospel. Whitefield is clear in his position on Election—

"The doctrine of our election, and free justification in Christ Jesus are daily more and more pressed upon my heart. They fill my soul with a holy fire and afford me great confidence in God my Saviour. I hope we shall catch fire from each other, and that there will be a holy emulation amongst us, who shall most debase man and exalt the Lord Jesus. Nothing but the doctrines of the Reformation can do this. All others leave free will in man and make him, in part at least, a saviour unto himself. My soul, come not thou near the secret of those who teach such things . . . I know Christ is all in all. Man is nothing; he hath a free will to go to hell but none to go to heaven, till God worketh in him to will and to do of His good pleasure. Oh, the excellency of the doctrine of election and of the saints' final perseverance! I am persuaded, till a man comes to believe and feel these important truths, he cannot come out of himself, but when convinced of these, and assured of their application to his own heart, he then walks by faith indeed! . . . Love, not fear, constrains him to obedience. I bless God, His Spirit has convinced me of our eternal election by the Father through the Son, of our free justification through faith in His blood, of our sanctification as the consequence of that, and of our final perseverance and glorification as the result of all. These I am persuaded God has joined together; these, neither men nor devils shall ever be able to put asunder. Was there any fitness foreseen in us, except a fitness for damnation? I believe not. No, God chose us from eternity, He called us in time, and I am persuaded will keep us from falling finally, till time shall be no more. Consider the Gospel in this view, and it appears a consistent scheme . . . Put them in mind of the freeness and eternity of God's electing love, and be instant with them to lay hold of the perfect righteousness of Jesus Christ by faith. Talk to them, oh, talk to them, even till mid-night, of the riches of His all-sufficient grace. Tell them, oh, tell them, what He has done for their souls and how earnestly He is now interceding for them in Heaven. Show them, in the map of the Word, the kingdoms of the upper world, and the transcendent glories of them; and assure them all shall be theirs if they believe on Jesus Christ with their whole hearts. Press them to believe on Him immediately! Intersperse prayers with your exhortations, and thereby call down fire from heaven, even the fire of the Holy Ghost,

To soften, sweeten and refine<br>
And melt them into love.

Speak every time, my dear brother, as if it was your last. Weep out, if possible, every argument, and as it were, compel them to cry, 'Behold how he loveth us!' Remember me, remember me, in your prayers." [12]

27

# UNCONDITIONAL ELECTION

**Isaac Backus** (1724-1806) was also an early Baptist preacher in America as well as one foremost among Baptist historians. He saw himself as a defender of the doctrines of Calvinism. In fact, he had one pamphlet entitled, The Doctrine of Particular Election and Final Perseverance, and another entitled, The Sovereign Decrees of God. His confession of faith prepared for the First Baptist Church in Middleboro in 1756 states, "God the Father, of His mere good pleasure from all eternity, hath chosen a number of poor lost men in Christ Jesus to eternal salvation." Backus himself stated:

> "In short, the main objections I ever heard against sovereign election and certain salvation by free grace alone appear to me to spring from this root, viz., Man who was flattered with the notion of being as gods still conceits that he has a power in himself to do as he pleases let that pleasure be to comply with or to disappoint God's designs; and therefore if they are not disposed at present to engage in his service that he must wait their leisure, and be ready, when ever they set about the work in good earnest to grant them the assistance of his grace and, if they improve it well unto the end, then to receive them to his glory." [13]

**John Newton** (1725-1807) was a sailor, slave trader, infidel, and finally by God's amazing grace, a devoted servant of Jesus Christ. Ordained a Church of England minister at the age of thirty-nine, Newton is probably best known for his hymn, "Amazing Grace." He states,

> "They who believe there is any power in man by nature, whereby he can turn to God, may contend for a

conditional election upon the foresight of faith and obedience; but while others dispute, let you and me admire; for we know that the Lord foresaw us (as we were) in the state utterly incapable either of believing or obeying, unless he was pleased to work in us to will and to do according to his own good pleasure.

"Further, when you are led (as I think you will be, if you are not already) to view the Calvinist doctrines in favourable light, be not afraid of embracing them, because there may be, perhaps, some objections, against the other side. We are poor weak creatures: and the clearing up of every difficulty is not what we are immediately called to, but rather to seek that light which may strengthen and feed our souls." [14]

**Andrew Fuller** (1754-1815) was an English Baptist and pastor at Soham and Kettering. Fuller was active in the formation of the Baptist Missionary Society (1792) and was a voluminous writer best known for his book, The Gospel Worthy of all Acceptation. The following quote is taken from Baptists and the Bible–"He made such substantial progress in his understanding of these doctrines that in 1785 he published his conclusions in this book. Fuller's main point in this writing is that it is the duty of all men (whether they are among the elect or not) to repent and believe the gospel. Therefore, those duties must be pressed upon all men by preachers of the gospel. All men are perverse and totally depraved. All men flee from God, and they are, therefore, justly condemned for refusing to do what God requires. That God in mercy elects some and makes provision for them does not lessen the obligation of all to believe. He states–
    'There is no contradiction between this peculiarity

of design in the death of Christ, and universal obligation on those who hear the gospel to believe in him, or universal invitation being addressed to them. If God, through the death of his Son, have promised salvation to all who comply with the gospel; and if there be no natural impossibility as to a compliance, nor an obstruction but that which arises from aversion of heart; exhortations and invitations to believe and be saved are consistent and our duty, as preachers of the Gospel, is to administer them, without any more regard to particular redemption than to election; both being secret things, which belong to the Lord our God, and which, however they be a rule to him, are none to us!' (Works, 2:374)

The Particular Baptist Foreign Mission Society was formed in 1792 in the home of one of his church members. Fuller was appointed secretary of the society and continued as such until his death in May of 1815." [15]

**William Carey** (1761-1834) has been named "The Father of Modern Missions." In 1792 he helped organize the English Baptist Missionary Society, and the next year he went to India as one of its first missionaries. Kenneth Good, in his book, <u>Are Baptists Calvinists?</u> states, "He went to India as a Particular Baptist and remained in that fellowship until he died. His convictions were those of Andrew Fuller, his loyal supporter in England." Erroll Hulse declares, "The group which associated with Andrew Fuller and included Pearce, Ryland . . . and Carey stood in the tradition of the 1689 Confession." [16]

In 1805 Carey drew up his "Form of Agreement," which gave direction to the brethren of the Mission of Serampore in their labors. The following statement is taken from the first paragraph: "We are sure that only those who are ordained to eternal life will believe, and that God alone can add to the church such as shall be saved. Nevertheless we cannot but observe with admiration that Paul, the great champion for the glorious doctrines of free and sovereign grace, was the most conspicuous for his personal zeal in the work of persuading men to be reconciled to God." [17]

**Luther Rice** (1783-1836) founded the "General Missionary Convention of the Baptist Denomination of the United States of America for Foreign Missions" and delighted in the doctrines of grace.. He said, "How absurd it is therefore to contend against the doctrine of election or the decrees of divine sovereignty. Let us not, however, become bitter against those who view this matter in a different light nor treat them in a supercilious manner. Rather let us be gentle towards all men. For who has made us to differ from what we once were? Who has removed the scales from our eyes? Or who has disposed us to embrace the truth?" [18]

**Adoniram Judson** (1788-1850) was another Baptist leader in the modern missionary movement. In 1829 Judson wrote a liturgy and creed for the Burman church. Point seven of the liturgy, in which "Particular Attributes and Actions of the Christian God" are described, says, "God, who pitied the sinful race of man, sent His only beloved Son into the world to save from sin and hell, who also sends the Holy Spirit to enable those to become disciples who were chosen before the world was and given to the Son, we worship." In the creed, Article 4, Judson writes, "God, originally knowing that mankind would fall and be ruined, did of His mercy select some of the race and did give them to His Son to save them from sin and hell." [19]

**Frances Wayland** (1796-1865) was a Baptist pastor, President of Brown University and the one whom Broadus acclaimed as "the most distinguished of all American educators." Again in Baptists and the Bible we read, "After his conversion, the doctrine of election, offensive to him earlier, became a source of great comfort.

> 'My mind at one time rebelled against the doctrine of election. It seemed to me like partiality. I now perceived that I had no claim whatever on God, but that if I were lost it was altogether my own fault, and that if I was saved, it must be purely a deed of unmerited grace. I saw that this very doctrine was my only hope of salvation, for if God had not sought me, I should never have sought him.'" [20]

In the book, By His Grace and For His Glory, Wayland is quoted on the subject of Unconditional Election:

> "God in infinite mercy 'has elected some to everlasting life and, by the influence of the Holy Spirit, rendered the word effectual to their salvation and sanctification.' Although salvation is honestly and sincerely offered to all, this offer in no way interferes 'with his gracious purpose to save by his sovereign mercy such as he may choose.'" [21]

**Basil Manly, Sr.** was one of the great founders of the Southern Baptist Convention. He was born in 1798 and would be used of God to give pastoral ministry to J. P. Boyce for the first ten years of Boyce's life. From the book Southern Baptist Sermons on Sovereignty and Responsibility, we read select parts of an overview on Manly's life: "From 1838-1855 Manly presided over the University of Alabama at Tuscaloosa. In addition to his settling the floundering institution on a solid basis during that time, he played the part of concertmaster in orchestrating the events that resulted in the call for a consultative convention of Baptists." "When the new convention was formed, Manly was elected as President of the Domestic Mission Board to be located in Marion, Alabama."

"His commitment to education prompted Manly to expend great amounts of energy upon the establishing of Southern Baptist Theological Seminary. He presided for several years over an ad hoc committee convened specifically for ascertaining whether the difficulties standing in the way of establishing a seminary were insuperable. When finally established, his own son, Basil Jr., and his former parishioner, J. P. Boyce, formed one half of the original faculty." "A polemical situation had arisen between the Tuscaloosa and the North River Associations in Alabama. The North River Association, under the leadership of David W. Andrews, had altered its confession on the doctrines of election and effectual calling so that a danger of susceptibility to Arminianism was very real. One church had even cast aside its entire confession to which an investigative council had responded:

'While the scriptures of the Old and New Testaments are the only authoritative standard of doctrine, and rule of duty, it is still deemed expedient to have summary statements or abstracts of principles, for the sake of distinctness.'

In an effort to reconcile both parties to the question, the council recommended adoption of a sermon preached by Basil Manly, Sr. All members stated candidly that the 'sentiments and doctrine . . . meet our cordial and entire approbation.'"

The following quotations are taken from this sermon by Manly. It is filled with a theology of God's absolute sovereignty being compatible with human responsibility.

"Let us not, then, give up either the doctrine of human activity and responsibility, or that of the divine sovereignty and efficiency. Why should they be thought inconsistent? Or why should those who cling to one be disposed to doubt, or disbelieve, or explain away, the other? If you cannot see the consistency of both, that does not prove them inconsistent."

"I will not multiply quotations; the current of scripture ascribes the incipient operation to God." 'I have loved thee with an everlasting love; therefore with lovingkindness have I drawn thee.' 'Ye have not chosen me, but I have chosen you, and ordained you, that ye should go and bring forth fruit.' 'Of his own will begat he us with the word of truth.' 'No man can come to me, except the Father which hath sent me draw him.' 'Which were born not of blood, nor of the will of the flesh, nor of the will of man, but of God.'"

"But how was it in your experience? Let us go back, in our consciousness, with this question: for, if there is a work of grace in us, that work is a subject of consciousness, to some extent. Now I ask any Christian man to say—did you go, irrespective of motive; go first to meet him and then he came to meet you? Did you, without a change of heart, resolve to change your own heart? And did this effort, self-determined, self-dependent, succeed? If so, the credit of the whole operation, the merit of the work belongs to you. The Christian heart replies,

'– no, Jesus sought me first.' Take a true believer away from theological creeds and technicalities, from the musty volumes of controversy and the arena of bitter strife, and there is but one voice on the subject; '–Not unto us, not unto us, but unto God be all the glory."

"How began that work, and who began it? Oh! if I had a tongue that could alarm the dead in their narrow hour, –and, for an audience the assembled universe; I would rejoice to shout the acclamations of Glory to their rightful object. It is all due to God who loved me first, and gave himself for me:–who, when I was guiltily disinclined to it, brought my unwilling heart to seek him. Then, and thus, it began; hence, it is of grace, not of works."

"Now, if God knows all things, he knows who will be saved. But, could God know who will be saved, if it were not capable of being seen, as certain. But if, in order to be saved, a divine operation is necessary, and the incipient part of that operation belongs to God, could he foreknow that the man would believe, unless he had a gracious purpose to work this operation in him, so that he might believe?"

"My brethren, however mysterious and incomprehensible it may be, that God chose a poor sinner like me–freely chose me, loved me, redeemed me, called me, justified me, and will glorify me–I will rejoice in the truth, and thank him for his free grace! O, where is boasting, then? Not at the feet of Jesus; not at the cross. It belongs not to that position."

"He is left to act freely, and as a matter of choice. In regard to salvation, so far from compelling a man,

# UNCONDITIONAL ELECTION

against his will, the very thing which God does is to
make him willing to act right; of his own choice, and
under sufficient motive. The Christian is willing, and
chooses to do right because a divine operation has made
him so. He feels free. . ."[22]

<u>W. B. Johnson</u>, the first president of the Southern Baptist Con-
vention (1845-1850), had summarized the Baptist doctrine of
salvation by affirming "the denomination to which I have the
honor to belong holds . . . the sovereignty of God in the provision
and application of the plan of salvation." [23]

We again borrow statements from Dr. Nettles' sketch of the
life of W. B. Johnson: "'No single individual had more to do
with determining the nature of the Southern Baptist Convention
than W. B. Johnson.' So states James M. Morton, Jr., in an
article in <u>Baptist History and Heritage</u>. That Johnson was the
first president of the Southern Baptist Convention surprised no
one who was familiar with his unparalleled qualifications. As
early as 1813, when Johnson was about thirty, he discussed with
Luther Rice the formation of a general body of Baptists to
support foreign missions. This discussion later bore fruit in the
formation of the General Missionary Convention, known more
familiarly as the Triennial Convention.

"Johnson, born in South Carolina in 1782, had a rich Baptist
background. He graduated from Brown University, taught
school, pastored churches in South Carolina and Georgia. In
1813 Johnson presided over the Savannah Baptist Society for
Foreign Missions.

"From 1817 till his death Johnson was in South Carolina.
Active and formative in associational work, he was one of those
men who, in 1821, worked together to draft a constitution in

founding the South Carolina Baptist state convention. In 1825, he was elected president of the South Carolina Baptist Convention, a position he held for twenty-eight years.

When, in 1845, division in the ranks of the General Missionary Convention became inevitable, Johnson, who served as president of that convention during the years 1841-1844, became a leading figure in the new organization for Baptists in the South. Not only was he elected president of the consultative convention which met in Augusta, May 1845, but, also, he was elected first president of the Southern Baptist Convention, a position he held until 1851."

"In a sermon preached by Johnson in 1822 before the Charleston Association he argues cogently that 'interest . . . in the benefits of the atonement' are imparted 'according to the righteous and sovereign will of God,' and indeed Christ died 'actually to redeem and introduce to glory . . . all who are his people.' This association, the first Baptist association in the South, having within its membership the first Southern Baptist church, was founded in 1751 and adopted as its confession of faith the Second London Confession of 1689. The association had maintained the Calvinism of the confession as a statement of Christian orthodoxy at least until the end of the nineteenth century." Three chapters of this historic doctrinal statement will help readers to understand the solid doctrinal roots of our Southern Baptist heritage.[24]

# UNCONDITIONAL ELECTION
## THE BAPTIST CONFESSION OF FAITH OF 1689

### Chapter 3 - OF GOD'S DECREE

1. God hath decreed in himself, from all eternity, by the most wise and holy counsel of his own will, freely and unchangeably, all things, whatsoever comes to pass;[a] yet so as thereby is God neither the author of sin nor hath fellowship with any therein;[b] nor is violence offered to the will of the creature, nor yet is the liberty or contingency of second causes taken away, but rather established;[c] in which appears his wisdom in disposing all things, and power and faithfulness in accomplishing his decree.[d]

a. Isaiah 46:10, Eph. 1:11, Heb. 6:17, Rom. 9:15, 18.  b. James 1:13, I John 1:5. c. Acts 4:27, 28, John 19:11. d. Num. 23:19, Eph. 1:3-5.

2. Although God knoweth whatsoever may or can come to pass, upon all supposed conditions,[e] yet hath he not decreed anything, because he foresaw it as future, or as that which would come to pass upon such conditions. [f]

e. Acts 15:18.  f. Romans 9:11, 13, 16, 18.

3. By the decree of God, for the manifestation of his glory, some men and angels are predestinated, or foreordained to eternal life through Jesus Christ,[g] to the praise of his glorious grace;[h] others being left to act in their sin to their just condemnation, to the praise of his glorious justice.[i]

g. I Tim. 5:21, Matt. 25:34. h. Eph. 1:5,6. i. Romans 9:22,23, Jude 4.

4. These angels and men thus predestinated and foreordained, are particularly and unchangeably designed, and their

number so certain and definite, that it cannot be either increased or diminished.[j]

j. II Tim. 2:19, John 13:18.

5. Those of mankind that are predestinated to life, God, before the foundation of the world was laid, according to his eternal and immutable purpose, and the secret counsel and good pleasure of his will, hath chosen in Christ unto everlasting glory, out of his mere free grace and love,[k] without any other thing in the creature as a condition or cause moving him thereunto.[l]

k. Eph. 1:4, 9, 11, Rom. 8:30, II Tim. 1:9, I Thess. 5:9.  l. Rom. 9:13, 16, Eph. 2:5, 12.

6. As God hath appointed the elect unto glory, so he hath, by the eternal and most free purpose of his will, foreordained all the means thereunto;[m] wherefore they who are elected, being fallen in Adam, are redeemed by Christ,[n] are effectually called unto faith in Christ, by his Spirit working in due season, are justified, adopted, sanctified,[o] and kept by his power through faith unto salvation;[p] neither are any other redeemed by Christ, or effectually called, justified, adopted, sanctified, and saved, but the elect only.[q]

m. I Peter 1:2, II Thess. 2:13.  n. I Thess. 5:9, 10.  o. Rom. 8:30, II Thess. 2:13.  p. I Peter 1:5.  q. John 10:26; 17:9, 6:64.

## Chapter 9 - OF FREE WILL

1. God hath indued the will of man with that natural liberty and power of acting upon choice, that it is neither forced, nor by any necessity of nature determined to do good or evil.[a]

a. Matt. 17:12, James 1:14, Deut. 30:19.

2. Man, in his state of innocency, had freedom and power to will and to do that which was good and well-pleasing to God,[b] but yet was unstable, so that he might fall from it.[c]

b. Ecclesiastes 7:29. c. Genesis 3:6.

3. Man, by his fall into a state of sin, hath wholly lost all ability of will to any spiritual good accompanying salvation;[d] so as a natural man, being altogether averse from that good, and dead in sin,[e] is not able by his own strength to convert himself, or to prepare himself thereunto.[f]

d. Romans 5:6; 8:7. e. Eph. 2:1,5. f. Titus 3:3-5, John 6:44.

4. When God converts a sinner, and translates him into the state of grace, he freeth him from his natural bondage under sin,[g] and by his grace alone enables him freely to will and to do that which is spiritually good;[h] yet so as that by reason of his remaining corruptions, he doth not perfectly, nor only will, that which is good, but doth also will that which is evil.[i]

g. Col. 1:13, John 8:36. h. Phil. 2:13. i. Romans 7:15, 18, 19, 21, 23.

5. This will of man is made perfectly and immutably free to good alone in the state of glory only.[j]

j. Eph. 4:13.

## Chapter 10 - OF EFFECTUAL CALLING

4. When God converts a sinner, and translates him into the state of appointed and accepted time, effectually to call,[a] by his Word and Spirit, out of that state of sin and death in which they

are by nature, to grace and salvation by Jesus Christ;[b] enlightening their minds spiritually and savingly to understand the things of God;[c] taking away their heart of stone, and giving unto them a heart of flesh:[d] renewing their wills, and by his almighty power determining them to that which is good, and effectually drawing them to Jesus Christ;[e] yet so as they come most freely, being made willing by his grace.[f]

a. Rom. 8:30; 11:7, Eph. 1:10, 11, II Thess. 2:13, 14. b. Eph. 2:1-6. c. Acts 26:18, Eph. 1:17, 18. d. Ezek. 36:26. e. Deut. 30:6, Ezek. 36:27, Eph. 1:19. f. Psalm 110:3, Song of Sol. 1:4.

This document is also referred to in the sections on Benjamin Keach, William Carey, and C. H. Spurgeon.

The following quotations are also taken from Johnson's sermon, "Love Characteristic of Deity," as delivered to the Charleston Association.

"One great object that Christ had in view, in undertaking the office of Mediator, was actually to redeem and introduce to glory, all believers in his name, all who are his people. In proof of this, the following scriptures will be found conclusive. 'And this is the Father's will which hath sent me, that of all which he hath given me, I should lose nothing, but should raise it up at the last day.' 'All that the Father giveth me shall come unto me, and him that cometh to me I will in no wise cast out.' 'It became him, for whom are all things, and by whom are all things, in bringing many sons unto glory, to make the Captain of their salvation perfect through sufferings.' 'Blessed be the God and Father of our Lord Jesus Christ, who hath blessed us with all spiritual blessings in heavenly places in Christ; according as he hath chosen us in him before the foundation of the world.' 'Christ loved the church and gave himself for it; that he might sanctify and cleanse it with the washing of water by the word; that he might present it to himself a glorious church.

"Paul, on this subject, speaking of the work as already done, presents us with a glorious chain, whose first link consists of the purpose of the eternal mind, and the last, of its accomplishment in ultimate glory. For, whom he, that is God, did foreknow, he also did predestinate to be conformed to the image of his Son, that he might be the first-born among many brethren. Moreover, whom he did predestinate, them he also called; and whom he called, them he also justified, and whom he justified, them he also glorified."

"To exhibit what has just been stated in relation to the destruction of the finally impenitent, with fuller force, and in a clearer point of view, let it be further observed, that the determination of God to recover his people, through the atonement of Jesus, in the manner in which the atonement has been stated in this discourse, does not exclude any of the human race from the enjoyment of God's love. In the sacrifice of Christ, an ample provision is made for the pardon of sin, on the most enlarged scale. Those who will not be benefited by it in their highest concerns, are only left in their state of rebellion, and in which without atonement, and its application, all would have been left—On those, who remain in this state, no injury is operated. They are not excluded from God's favour by any arbitrary power in him. They exclude themselves by their own act–by their own voluntary opposition to him, and persevering rejection of the only plan by which they can be saved. God, as the righteous Judge, will only inflict on them that punishment, to which they expose themselves, under circumstances of most aggravated guilt. Jesus is freely exhibited to them. Without money, and without price, irrespective of merit in them, and freed from all conditions on their part, they are invited, encouraged, commanded to believe in Christ, and assured that believing in his name, they shall have life and be eternally saved. For the exercise of this faith, they have the natural ability. For with the same ability that they disbelieve, they can believe. Their hearts are enmity against God. Under the influence of this enmity, they exercise the ability which they possess, in refusing to accept Jesus. They refuse to exercise faith in his name. They treat the offer of his mercy with neglect, if not with contempt. God is under no obligation to exert his transforming influence upon their hearts, to bring them to the exercise of faith. Where then is the injustice or malevolence in leaving them to the awful result of their deliberate choice? And if it seem good to the all-perfect mind to leave them in this state, who is he that shall reply against God?" [25]

**R. B. C. Howell**, the second president of the S. B. C. (1851-1858), held the same views of God's eternal purpose. "His book, The Covenants, begins with the sentence, 'Salvation through Jesus Christ, is according to the determinate counsel, and foreknowledge of God.' Naturally, then, 'the covenant of redemption was

...brought into being before the creation of the world' by the triune God for the salvation of men while maintaining the 'purity, justice, and honor alike, of all the persons of the adorable Trinity.' This covenant then secures 'your enlightenment, your regeneration, and your sanctification' as well." [26]

Howell gave staunch leadership to Baptists in the South while pastoring the First Baptist Church of Nashville beginning in 1835. He faced conflict valiantly as three theological debates threatened the Biblical positions of those churches. Those debates were over Campbellism, hyper-Calvinism, and local church autonomy–Dr. Nettles writes these words concerning Howell's fierce debate with hyper-Calvinism:

"His second conflict was with the anti-missionary forces of Tennessee and northern Alabama. These forces responded negatively to the formation of the General Missionary Convention and the work of its most notable agent, Luther Rice, referring to him as a "Modern Tetzel." In addition to the ecclesiological objections they held toward centralized organizations, they discountenanced some of the methods used by the agents, declaring them to be Arminian in methodology, thus denying their Calvinistic heritage. Eventually, however, the anti-mission society movement degenerated into pure hyper-Calvinism and denied the validity of giving a free offer of the gospel to all men, railed against theological education, and viewed the Bible societies as totally unwarranted by the Word of God. Such an unfortunate confrontation with forces ostensibly affirming Calvinistic soteriology might prompt an overreaction in the faint-hearted and result in a dismissal of all references to the doctrines of grace. Not so with Howell, as indicated by the present reprint. Moreover, in his book entitled The Covenants, Howell discusses the covenant of redemption and the prerogative of God to refuse to redeem any of his rebellious creatures. Howell concludes:

> 'The whole arrangement was, therefore, of his own sovereign grace, uninfluenced by human merit. But this conclusion is not only inferrable from the facts before you. His entire sovereignty in this whole transaction is expressly affirmed in his word:–"not by works of righteousness which we have done, but according to his mercy he saved us, by the washing (purifying) of regeneration, and the renewing of the Holy Ghost; which he shed on us abundantly through Jesus Christ our Savior; that being justified by his grace, we should be made heirs, according to the hope of eternal life"' [27]

"In his book, <u>The Way of Salvation</u>, Howell supports his discussion of "Persevering in Grace" by appealing to the whole body of the doctrines of grace.

> "Now if in Christ Jesus you were from the beginning chosen, to salvation, and to secure it you have been actually called, and endowed with faith, and sanctification; if through him you have been pardoned and the claims of the law against you fully satisfied; if you are recognized, and proclaimed heirs with Christ of the heavenly inheritance; if you already have everlasting life; and have his glorious promise–'Because I live ye shall live also;' what can we conclude but that your connection with Christ secures effectually, your final and complete salvation."[28]

**Richard Fuller** was the third president of the S. B. C., from 1859 to 1864. From Dr. Nettles we learn that Fuller "continued the tradition of Calvinistic presidents of the Southern Baptist

Convention. His understanding and defense of the congruence between divine predestination and human responsibility finds admirable statement in his sermon, 'Predestination,' in the book <u>Baptist Doctrine</u>. Fuller has little patience with those 'theological partisans' who treat scriptures as lawyers treat 'witnesses whose evidence damages their cause.' They brow-beat the clearest passages in an effort to 'extort from them a testimony they will not and cannot give.' The language of predestination, however, is so clear as to admit of no debate. Fuller concludes that a rejection of predestination is 'wholly untenable.' Not only does such rejection solve no difficulty, 'it stultifies our reason, it is practical atheism, and it contradicts the express assertions of the Bible.'"[29] Here are a few choice pieces from his sermon called "Predestination":

> "My brethren, the guide, the arbiter we seek is before us. It is God himself. He understands fully his decrees; he also comprehends man's free agency; and he declares as we have seen, that all our speculations are wrong; that both these doctrines are true; and, of course, that there is no discrepancy between them. I have shown that it is impossible for us to reject either of these great truths, and it is equally impossible for our minds to reconcile them. But here, as everywhere, faith must come to our aid, teaching us to repose unquestioningly upon God's veracity; reminding us that 'secret things belong unto the Lord our God; . . .'

> "Do you receive the doctrine of predestination? Certainly. To reject it, I would have to stultify my intellect, to discard prophecy, which is based upon this truth, to abjure the unequivocal teachings of the Bible, to believe that God has abandoned the earth to chance

and disorder, and to plunge into I know not what absurdities. Well, then you do not receive the doctrine of man's free agency. Indeed I do; for otherwise I must renounce my own distinct consciousness, I must disbelieve the Scriptures, I must make God the author and yet the punisher of sin, I must precipitate myself into I know not what absurdities. I embrace both doctrines. Nay, more; I see clearly that if I reject either of these great truths and cling to the other, it will tow me away into fathomless depths of folly and impiety. But, how do you reconcile these two doctrines? Reconcile! I do not reconcile them at all. I am not required to reconcile them. Who made me judge and reconciler of God's acts and attributes and clearly revealed testimonies? No, my brethren; let us rather with Job exclaim, 'Behold I am vile, what shall I answer thee? I will lay my hand upon my mouth. Once have I spoken, but I will not answer, yea, twice, but I will proceed no farther.'" [30]

**J. L. Dagg** (1794-1884) truly was a giant among Baptist theologians of America. William Cathcart, the Baptist historian, said, "Among the most distinguished men of the Baptist denomination in the United States, Dr. Dagg of right holds a place." In the early days of the Southern Baptist Convention, Dagg served on the Executive Committee of the Georgia Baptist Convention, was elected to the Constitution Committee of the Southern Baptist Convention at its first meeting in Augusta, Georgia in 1844, and in 1879 was asked to draw up a catechism for use in Southern Baptist churches (which he was unable to do because of declining health). He was also president of Haddington College, Alabama Female Athenaeum, and Mercer University. Dagg deserves to be recognized as the first writing Southern Baptist systematic theologian. His "Manual of Theology" was first published in 1857, twenty-five years before J. P. Boyce's <u>Abstract of Systematic Theology</u>. In fact, Boyce used Dagg's work as a textbook for the first ten years of Southern Seminary's existence. John A. Broadus said, "Dr. Dagg was a man of great ability and lovable character. His works are worthy of a thorough study." [31]

Paige Patterson, President of the Criswell Center for Biblical Studies said, "If one wishes to know what most Baptists believed during the formative days of the Southern Baptist Convention, he will discover it in this volume. With remarkable insight, John Leadley Dagg–pastor, theologian, evangelist, teacher, and college president–presents the essence of biblical truth in a thoroughly readable, yet scholarly, presentation. The indefatigable spirit of this early Baptist thinker, who suffered numerous physical reversals, glows with experiential insight into the crucial doctrines honored by Baptists everywhere. Every pastor, professor, and seminary student should avail himself of the opportunity to become acquainted with one of the most sublime of our Baptist fathers." [32]

The following is taken from Dagg's "Manual of Theology."

## SOVEREIGNTY OF GRACE

God bestows the blessings of his grace, not according to the works of the recipient but according to his own sovereign pleasure. God is sovereign in doing what he pleases, uncontrolled by any other being. "He doth according to his will, in the armies of heaven, and among the inhabitants of the earth, and none can stay his hand, or say unto him: 'What doest thou?' No superior being exists, who can dictate to Jehovah what he should do, or hinder him from the execution of his pleasure, or call him to account for anything that he has done. Sovereignty is to be distinguished from arbitrariness. In the latter, the will of the agent directs the action, without reference to a wise or good pleasure. His pleasure is good, because it is always directed to his own perfections.

## ELECTION

All who will finally be saved, were chosen to salvation by God the Father, before the foundation of the world, and given to Jesus Christ in the Covenant of Grace. The doctrine of election encounters strong opposition in the hearts of men, and it is therefore necessary to examine thoroughly its claim to our belief. As it relates to an act of the divine mind, no proof of its truth can be equal to the testimony of the Scriptures. Let us receive their teachings on the subject without hesitation or distrust; and let us require every preconceived opinion of ours, and all our carnal reasonings, to bow before the authority of God's holy word. The Scriptures clearly teach, that God has an elect chosen people. "Who shall lay any thing to the charge of God's elect." "Elect according to the foreknowledge of God." "Shall not God avenge his own elect." "Ye are a chosen generation." "God hath chosen you to salvation." "According as he hath chosen us in Christ." Whatever may have been our prejudices against the doctrine of election as held and taught by some ministers of religion, it is undeniable, that, in some sense, the doctrine

49

is found in the Bible: and we cannot reject it, without rejecting that inspired book. We are bound by the authority of God, to receive the doctrine; and nothing remains, but that we should make an honest effort to understand it, just as it is taught in the sacred volume. The Scriptures teach expressly, that God's people are chosen to salvation. "Beloved, we are bound to give thanks always to God for you, because he hath from the beginning chosen you to salvation."

The election to salvation is shown by the words of Paul in Romans 9:6 and 11:5 to be different from this national election: "They are not all Israel that are of Israel." And "There is a remnant according to the election of grace." The national election comprehended all Israel, according to the flesh: but the election of grace included those only who will finally be saved. It is not a choice merely to the means of salvation, for these were granted to all the nation of Israel: but it was a choice to salvation itself, and therefore respected the "remnant" and not the whole nation.

The Scriptures teach that election is of grace, and not of works. "Not of works, lest any man should boast:" "and if it be of works, then grace is no more grace." The subject is illustrated by the case of Jacob and Esau, of whom Jacob was chosen, before the children had done either good or evil; and in applying this illustration, Paul says: "That the purpose of God according to election might stand: not of works, but of him that calleth." In the last day, God will discriminate between the righteous and the wicked, according to their works: and it was the eternal purpose of God, that this discrimination should then be made on that ground; but the purpose of God includes an earlier discrimination made in effectual calling; whence we read of those who are "the called according to his purpose."

This actual separation of God's people from the rest of mankind, made in their effectual calling, is like everything which he does, the fulfillment of his eternal purpose. "He worketh all things after the counsel of his will:" and "known unto him are all his works from the beginning." The purpose to effect this first actual discrimination, is God's election; and the ground of the discrimination when it actually takes place, is nothing different from that of the purpose to discriminate; that is, it is the ground of election.

From the views which have been presented, it necessarily follows, that election is not on the ground of foreseen faith or obedience. The Scriptures teach that election is according to the foreknowledge of God. We are, however, not to understand the foreknowledge here mentioned, to be foreknowledge of faith or good works. Faith and good works do not exist, before the grace consequent on election begins to be bestowed; and therefore a foresight of them is impossible. Moreover, the objects of this divine foreknowledge are the persons of the elect, and not their faith or good works. "Whom he foreknew, them he also did predestinate." In this foreknowledge of person, according to the Scripture use of terms, a peculiar regard to them is implied. It is said, "Hath God cast away his people, whom he foreknew?" If simple knowledge, without any peculiar regard, were all that is here implied, it would be equally true that God foreknew the heathen nations, as well as the nation of Israel. [33]

In <u>Baptists and the Bible</u> we read: "The enduring respect that Dagg enjoyed among Southern Baptists and the implicit acquiescence of Baptist leadership to his theological viewpoint is quite plainly revealed in an action taken at the Southern Baptist Convention in 1879. W. H. Whitsitt offered the following resolutions:

> Resolved, That a catechism be drawn up, containing the substance of the Christian religion, for the instruction of children and servants, and that brother John L. Dagg be desired to draw it up.

> Resolved, That brethren Peter, Mell, Winkler, Gambrell and Boyce be requested to assist brother Dagg in this work, in the capacity of a Committee of Revision.

> Resolved, That in case brother Dagg is unable to accede to the request of the Convention, the brethren of the Committee of Revision be desired to draw up the said catechism.

> Resolved, That the brethren in question be desired to publish the said catechism as soon as convenient after it is prepared" (SBC Annual, 1879 p. 15).

The following morning at ten o'clock the resolutions were discussed and passed unanimously. Evidently Dagg, in failing health, was unable to fulfill this assignment. Subsequent Convention annuals make no mention of it, and E. C. Starr in his Baptist bibliography does not list a catechism among the works of Dagg. Further evidence that Dagg did not write this catechism appears from the fact that in 1891 John Broadus was commissioned by the new Sunday School Board to write a catechism (because one was still not available). Nevertheless, this convention action of 1879 stands as an eloquent testimony to the widespread theological respect enjoyed by J. L. Dagg. In the South, Dagg's volumes eventually replaced those of Francis Wayland as texts in Baptist colleges. John A. Broadus, in his Memoirs of James P. Boyce, indicates his personal estimation of Dagg's contribution.

'Dr. Dagg was a man of great ability and lovable character. His works are worthy of thorough study, especially his small volume 'A Manual of Theology' (American Baptist Publication Society), which is remarkable for clear statement of the profoundest truths, and for devotional sweetness. The writer of this Memoir may be pardoned for bearing witness that after toiling much, in his early years, as a pastor, over Knapp and Turrettin, Dwight and Andrew Fuller, and other elaborate theologians, he found this manual a delight, and has felt through life the pleasing impulse it gave to theological inquiry and reflection.'" [34]

**P. H. Mell** (1814-1888) was president of the Southern Baptist Convention for seventeen years and held more official positions in Baptist life than any other Southern Baptist in history. He also was professor of Greek and Latin at Mercer University in Georgia. He also is clear on the subject of Election:

"The elect are chosen, not because God foresees faith and good works in them; but in part that they might have faith and might perform good works: or, in the language of the Confession of Faith, quoted by our author: 'God hath chosen them in Christ, unto everlasting glory, out of his mere free grace and love, without any foresight of faith or good works, or perseverance in either of them or any other thing in the creature, as conditions or causes moving him thereunto.' God's act in electing some and not others is to be resolved into his sovereign will. He hath mercy on whom he will have mercy, and whom he will he hardeneth (Rom. 9:18). While by an immutable decree He has made all things in time fixed and sure, all this occurs in perfect consistency with the free agency of the creature, and God is not the author of sin. The elect are, by the influence of sovereign grace, made willing in the day of God's power and those not elected have no active principle of disobedience imparted to them, and feel no restraint upon their wills–they are simply passed by, and permitted to follow the inclinations of their own hearts. While they work out God's purposes, they do it unconsciously and wickedly. 'Him (Christ) being delivered by the determinate counsel and foreknowledge of God, ye have taken and by wicked hands have crucified and slain. (Acts 2:23).'" [35]

Dr. Nettles gives the following comments in the beginning of Mell's reprinted book A Southern Baptist Looks at Predestination–"Seeing election and reprobation as only two particular manifestations of the comprehensive sovereignty of God, he expressed their essence and relationship in the following way:

'In reference to men, predestination is divided into two parts: first, as it relates to the elect, and second, as it relates to the non-elect. Having decreed to create a world, and to people it with beings who would voluntarily sin against him, he determined from eternity to save some, and to leave others to perish in their sins. 'Willing to show his wrath, and to make his power known,' He 'endured with much longsuffering' these as 'the vessels of wrath fitted to destruction;' and that he might make known the riches of his glory on those as 'the vessels of mercy which he had afore prepared unto glory.' Romans 9:22,23.

'To carry out his purpose of grace, he chose some to holiness and eternal life, entered, for their sake, into the Covenant of Redemption with the Son and the Holy Ghost, appointed his Son as their substitute, to suffer in their stead, and having died to rise again, and appear as their advocate before his throne, appointed all the intermediate means necessary and, by an infallible decree, made their salvation sure. Those, 'whose names are not written in the book of life' (Rev. 20:15), who are 'appointed to wrath' (I Thess. 5:9), who were 'before of old ordained to condemnation' (Jude 4) who would 'stumble at the word, being disobedient, whereunto also they were appointed' (I Peter 2:8), he determined to leave in their sins, and to endure them with much longsuffering as vessels of wrath fitted to destruction.' (Rev. P. H. Mell, Predestination and the Saints' Perseverance Stated and Defended. Charleston: Southern Baptist Publication Society, 1851, pp. 26-27.)

"His love for and exposition of these truths were not forsaken in later life. The last sermon he ever preached, December 12, 1887, dealt with divine election. His text was II Thessalonians 2:13, 14:

# UNCONDITIONAL ELECTION

'But we are bound to give thanks always to God for you, brethren beloved of the Lord, because God hath from the beginning chosen you to salvation through sanctification of the Spirit and belief of the truth: Whereunto he called you by our gospel, to the obtaining of the glory of our Lord Jesus Christ.'

"Mell died in his home, January 26, 1888. At the Southern Baptist Convention session in 1888, the Foreign Mission Board presented a memorial tribute to Mell. The introductory paragraph captured their estimation of his traits and influence.

'The late President of the Southern Baptist Convention will be long remembered. His erect figure, angular features, keen eye, concise speech, his incisive thoughts, cogent logic, unyielding orthodoxy, commanding address, all represented a type of manhood which impresses indelibly even as steel makes cuts into granite not to be worn away by the waves of time.' (Life of Patrick Hues Mell, p. 255) "[36]


<u>J. P. Boyce</u> (1827-1888) was founder and first president of the Southern Baptist Theological Seminary (Louisville, Kentucky). He was also president of the Southern Baptist Convention (1872-1879, 1888). He believed in Unconditional Election and is regarded as one of the outstanding Baptist theologians of the nineteenth century.

His <u>Abstract of Systematic Theology</u> has been republished and we are given his remarks on Unconditional Election from his sermon by that title. "The theory of Calvinists as to election is that <u>God</u> (not man) <u>of His own purpose</u> (in accordance with His will, and not from any obligation to men, nor because of any will of man), <u>has from eternity</u> (the period of God's action, not

56

in time in which man acts), <u>determined to save</u> (not has actually saved, but simply determined so to do, and to save, not merely to confer gospel or church privileges upon) <u>a definite number of mankind</u> (not the whole race, nor indefinitely, merely some of them, nor indefinitely a certain proportionate part, but a definite number), <u>as individuals</u> (not the whole or part of the race, nor of a nation, nor of a church, nor of a class, as of believers or the pious; but individuals), <u>not for or because of any merit or work of theirs, nor of any value to him of them</u> (not for their good works, or their holiness or excellence, or their faith, or their spiritual sanctification although the choice is to a salvation attained through faith and sanctification; nor for their value to him, though their salvation tends greatly to the manifested glory of his grace); <u>but of good pleasure</u> simply because he was pleased so to choose." [37]

Rev. E. E. Folk, in the "Baptist Reflector" commented on Boyce's abilities and fruits as a teacher of theology: "He was a great teacher. He could get more hard, solid study out of a boy than any teacher whose classes we ever had the privilege of attending, with possibly one or two exceptions. You had to know your Systematic Theology, or you could not recite it to Dr. Boyce. And though the young men were generally rank Arminians when they came to the seminary, few went through this course under him without being converted to his strong Calvinistic views." [38]

"Rev. F. D. Hale, also pastor in Louisville, spoke of Dr. Boyce's silent influence over him as a student. When he began Boyce's Systematic Theology, it threw him into great perplexity as to doctrine. But he found it all of inestimable value. He had learned to have more faith in God and to take in the system of Christianity as a whole; and he had gained such a firm hold of the old doctrines of grace as he never had before, by standing under Dr. Boyce. He had also learned at his feet to love the work, and to sympathize with lost souls. He had a joy, a zeal, a hope, a faith, and a love for the gospel he would never have had but for Dr. Boyce." [39]

Boyce compiled "A Brief Catechism of Bible Doctrine," and the report from the Sunday School Board in 1864 lists his Catechism as one of its publications. Ten thousand of these catechisms were in print within a four-month period in 1864. [40] The following two sections are taken from Boyce's Catechism. The section entitled "The Offer of Salvation" is given in addition to the section on "Election" to show how evangelism and missions are compatible with the doctrine of election. [41]

THE OFFER OF SALVATION

Q. (1) To whom does God offer the salvation in Jesus?
A.　　He has ordered it to be offered to every creature.

Q. (2) Upon what conditions?
A　　Upon that of repentance and faith.

Q. (3) Are not these terms easy?
A.　　They are so easy that all who refuse are without excuse.

Q. (4) Do all men accept them?
A.　　They do not; they universally reject them where left without Divine influence.

Q. (5) Has God thus left all mankind?
A.　　He has not; but effectually calls many to the knowledge and belief of His truth.

Q. (6) What agent accomplished this work?

**A.** The Holy Spirit.

**Q.** (7) Do those who accept the Gospel deserve any reward for so doing?

**A.** No, for their acceptance is entirely due to the grace of God.

**Q.** (8) How will God punish those who reject it?

**A.** Far more severely than He will those who have never heard it.

**Q.** (9) Upon what grounds will he punish any who have not heard the gospel?

**A.** Because they, too, are sinners, and have disobeyed the law of God written in their hearts and in nature.

ELECTION

**Q.** (1) What name is given to those whom God effactually calls to salvation?

**A.** They are called the elect or the chosen ones of God.

**Q.** (2) Why are they so called?

**A.** Because God, before the foundation of the world, chose them unto salvation through Christ Jesus.

**Q.** (3) Did God make this choice because He foresaw that these persons would be pious and good people?

**A.** He did not, for the goodness and piety of any are due to the influences of the Spirit.

**Q.** (4) Was it, then, because He foresaw that they would believe?

**A.** On the contrary, it is through His choice that

they are led to believe.

**Q.** (5) What, then was the ground of that choice?

**A.** His own sovereign will.

**Q.** (6) How may we know if we be of the Elect of God?

**A.** Only by perceiving that the Holy Spirit has led us to repentance and faith and loving obedience to God.

**Q.** (7) Ought we not diligently to watch for such assurance of our calling and election?

**A.** Yes; and besides this we ought to pray to God to give His Spirit thus to work in us.

**John A. Broadus** (1827-1895) pastored the Baptist church in Charlottesville, Virginia until he devoted his life's labours to education. He assisted J. P. Boyce in organizing Southern Baptist Theological Seminary at Greenville, South Carolina in 1859, where he became professor of New Testament Interpretation and Homiletics. After the seminary had relocated in Louisville, Kentucky, he became president in 1888. Moyer spoke this of him—"A man of consummate scholarship, deep piety, wielding influence for righteousness second to no man of his generation." [42]

In describing the Calvinism of Dr. James P. Boyce, Broadus defined it as follows: "It was a great privilege to be directed and upborne by such a teacher in studying that exalted system of Pauline truth which is technically called Calvinism, which compels the earnest student to profound thinking, and when pursued with a combination of systematic thought and fervent experience, makes him at home among the most inspiring and ennobling views of God and the universe He has made." [43]

Again, Broadus speaks of Boyce's book <u>Abstract of Systematic Theology</u>:

> "The chief emphasis in this work is laid on the doctrine of God rather than on that of man. We give extracts from two notices which this work received at the time. The "Standard" of Chicago, a singularly able and judicious paper, points out carefully and correctly the peculiarities of the work, as designed for the text book in class instruction, and as omitting certain subjects commonly included in theological treatises. It then proceeds as follows: '–As a theologian Dr. Boyce is not afraid to be found 'in the old paths;' he is conservative, and eminently Scriptural. He treats with great fairness those whose view upon various points discussed he declines to accept, yet in his own teaching is decidedly Calvinistic, after the model of 'the old divines.' Difficulties, as connected with such doctrines as the Federal Headship of Adam, Election, and the Atonement, he aims to meet, evidently, not so as to silence the controversialist, but so as to help the honest inquirer.'

> "Dr. Boyce's work is, indeed, as these newspaper notices have said, thoroughly in accord with the system of theological opinion commonly called Calvinism. This is believed by many of us to be really the teaching of the Apostle Paul, as elaborated by Augustine, and systematized and defended by Calvin. It is a body of truth that compels men to think, –in itself a great advantage. The objections to it are believed to grow out of either misapprehension, or misapplication through wrong inferences. Men assume predestination and

election, and then deny human freedom and responsibility; or they assume freedom and accountability, and then deny predestination and election,—in either case because they cannot fully reconcile these two sides of theological truth; thus making our capacity to harmonize things the limit of possible truth, and the criterion of Scripture interpretation." [44]

Perhaps the Southern Baptist attitude toward the doctrines of grace in the first eighty years finds its most succinct summary in a letter written by John A. Broadus from Europe about his impressions in Geneva:

"The people who sneer at what is called Calvinism might as well sneer at Mount Blanc. We are not in the least bound to defend all of Calvin's opinions or actions, but I do not see how anyone who really understands the Greek of the Apostle Paul or the Latin of Calvin or Turretin can fail to see that the latter did but interpret and formulate substantially what the former teaches." [45]

**C. H. Spurgeon**, (1834-1892) the great "Prince of Preachers," pastored the Metropolitan Tabernacle of London. Moyer describes Spurgeon as an "ardent evangelical, a staunch Baptist, and a Calvinist."[46] He once said, "We only use the term 'Calvinism' for shortness. That doctrine which is called 'Calvinism' did not spring from Calvin; we believe that it sprang from the great founder of all truth. Perhaps Calvin himself derived it mainly from the writing of Augustine. Augustine obtained his views, without doubt, through the Holy Spirit of God, from diligent study of the writings of Paul, and Paul received them from the Holy Ghost and from Jesus Christ, the great founder of the Christian Church. We use the term then, not because we impute an extraordinary importance to Calvin's having taught these doctrines. We would be just as willing to call them by any other name, if we could be as consistent with the fact." Spurgeon went on to say, "The old truths that Calvin preached, that Augustine preached, is the truth that I preach today, or else I would be false to my conscience and my God. I cannot shape truth; I know of no such thing as paring off the rough edges of a doctrine. John Knox's gospel is my gospel. And that gospel which thundered through Scotland must thunder through England again." [47]

Again he states, "THIS IS A FACT. Men say they do not like the doctrine of election. Verily, I do not want them to; but is it not a fact that God has elected some? Ask an Arminian brother about election, and at once his eye turns fiercely upon you, and he begins to get angry, he can't bear it; it is a horrible thing, like a war-cry to him, and he begins to sharpen the knife of controversy at once. But say to him, 'Ah, brother! was it not the Lord who called you out of your natural state, and made you what you are?' 'Oh, yes,' he says, 'I quite agree with you there.' Now, put this question to him: What do you think is the reason why one man has been converted, and not another? 'Oh,' he says, 'the Spirit of God has been at work in this man.' 'Well, then, my brother, the fact is, that God does treat one man better than another; and is there anything wonderful in this fact?' It is a fact we recognize every day." [48]

Beginning a sermon on Romans 8:29, Spurgeon said, "It was most natural therefore that a deep spiritual experience should bring him to a clean perception of the doctrines of grace. For such an experience is a school in which alone those great truths are effectually learned. A lack of depth in the inner life accounts for most of the doctrinal error in the church. Sound conviction of sin, deep humiliation on account of it, and a sense of utter weakness and unworthiness naturally conduct the mind to the belief of the doctrines of grace, while shallowness in these matters leaves a man content with superficial creed. Those teachings which are commonly called Calvinist doctrines are usually most beloved and best received by those who have much conflict of soul and so have learned the strength of corruption and necessity of grace." [49]

From <u>Baptists and The Bible</u> we read, "in 1857 *The Texas Baptist* printed a description of Spurgeon as recorded by the London correspondent of the *Banner and Advocate*. Spurgeon was not yet twenty-three years old.

'Mr. Spurgeon is of the middle size–thick set in figure, with a deep, capacious chest, and a throat, and tongue, and lip, all formed for vehement oratory. His hair is black, over a tolerably wide forehead; his eyes dark and deep-set . . . He reads the Psalm abruptly; he prays with startling rapidity . . . Then comes an exposition of the chapter. What a torrent of words! What striking remarks, quaint and pithy! And how well he knows his Bible! It is not a lecture. The English will not stand that. But it is a rapid, running commentary, which in my mind, when well done, is the perfection of an expository reading before, and as preparatory to the sermon. Next comes the sermon itself . . . Listen, tho, to his language. How thoroughly English, vernacular: scarce a Latinized or Greek borrowed terms. Is it any wonder with this, and the rich, full, old doctrine of the Puritan age–election, defended, asserted, sovereign grace vindicated and glorified; Christ set forth as crucified and slain, pictures, anecdotes–that, in spite of extravagances and much of self, the common people hear him gladly ... He does take liberties with his audience; he does deal too much in stimulants; but anything better than these myriads of London allowed to perish unwarned, and anything better than that miserable negation of truth, which our younger preachers are setting forth as a new and better gospel. Spurgeon preaches the doctrine of grace with great courage and fullness: and like Paul, like Whitefield, like Berridge, and Romaine, he freely invites all to our Saviour.'" [50]

Again Spurgeon stated,

"And I have my own private opinion that there is no such thing as preaching Christ and Him crucified, unless you preach what now-a-days is called Calvinism. I have my own ideas, and those I always state boldly. It is a nickname to call it Calvinism; Calvinism is the gospel, and nothing else. I do not believe we preach the gospel, if we do not preach justification by faith without works; not unless we preach the sovereignty of God in his dispensation of grace; not unless we exalt the electing, unchangeable, eternal, immutable, conquering love of Jehovah; nor do I think we can preach the gospel, unless we base it upon the peculiar redemption which Christ made for his elect and chosen people; nor can I comprehend a gospel which lets saints fall away after they are called." [51]

Spurgeon married the doctrine of Election with soulwinning fervor in saying,

"What shall I say to you who are Christians, but this, do for the sake of this grace–show your gratitude, live more like your Master, and live more in God's service. Seek to spend and be spent in Him. Nothing can make a man work for Christ like free grace; and those who believe this doctrine of free grace and yet are idle, must surely hold the truth in unrighteousness, for there is no principle so active, so impulsive as this.

> 'Loved of my God, for Him again
> With love intense I'd burn:
> Chosen of Thee ere time began,
> I'd choose Thee in return.'

Finally, Christian, never give up on any sinner. Never think that any man is beyond salvation. I charge you by the solemn thought that God looketh for nothing in man, and saveth only according to the sweet counsels of His own will, bring every man you meet with before God in prayer, plead with every man, preach Christ to every man, tell every man that Christ can save, tell that sinner that whatever there may not be in him, Christ's power is still the same, that His arm is not shortened neither is his ear heavy; and spread ye the glad news that it is not of the will of man, nor blood, nor birth, but by the power of HIS mighty works this morning through Jesus Christ our Lord." [52]

Erroll Hulse has stated, "C. H. Spurgeon would have had little time for the spineless and uninspiring leadership so much in evidence today. He felt strongly about doctrine. At the commencement of his ministry in London he published the 1689 Confession, heartily commending it to his flock. 'This little volume,' he wrote in the foreword, 'is not issued as an authoritative rule, or code of faith, whereby you are to be fettered, but as an assistance to you in controversy, a confirmation in faith, and a means of edification in righteousness. Here the younger members of our church will have a body of divinity in small compass, and by means of the Scriptural proofs, will be ready to give a reason for the hope that is in them.'" [53]

**B. H. Carroll** (1843-1914) was the founder and first president of Southwestern Baptist Theological Seminary. He was converted in 1865 following a bitter struggle with skepticism. This pastor, educator, and denominational leader had great influence among Southern Baptists. His best-known work is <u>An Interpretation of English Bible</u>. He gives helpful insight into "Election" with the following statement:

"The last clause of Acts 13:48, which reads thusly: 'As many as were ordained to eternal life, believed,' needs some explanation. When I was a young fellow and had not imbibed the doctrine of predestination, I wanted that to read, 'And as many as believed were ordained to eternal life.' Perhaps that is the way you want to interpret it. Brother Broadus said, 'Let the Scripture mean what it wants to mean, and you let that passage stand–ordination to precede eternal life. Ordination to eternal life takes place in eternity.' Paul, in Romans 8, gives us the order. Many modern people do not believe it. We seldom ever hear anybody preach a sermon on it. I heard a strong preacher once say, 'I just can't believe it.' Romans 8:29 reads, 'For whom he did foreknow, he also foreordained to be conformed to the image of his Son . . . and whom he foreordained, them he also called: and whom he called, them he also justified.' Justification comes at believing. So unless that passage reads, 'As many as were ordained to eternal life believed,' it would break Paul's chain all to pieces.

Settle it in your mind that salvation commences with God, and not man." [54]

Carroll, speaking on the subject of "foreknowledge" in I Peter, told the following story–

"When I was a young preacher, a Baptist preacher who was a good man, but Arminian in his theology, preached a sermon on 'Election.' He said, 'Election is according to the foreknowledge of God. God foreknew that certain men would repent and believe. And having before seen that they would repent and believe, he elected them. When he got through, I told him that the New Testament use of 'foreknowledge' was almost equivalent to predestination and that any Greek scholar would tell him so and that election was not based on any foreseen goodness in man or any foreseen faith or repentance in man, but that repentance and faith proceed from election and not election from them. So what Paul means by 'foreknowledge' is just about the same as predestination–that in eternity, God determined and elected according to that predestination." [55]

The following information will be an aid in understanding Carroll's position on the word "foreknowledge." It is taken from a work by Arthur C. Custance, The Sovereignty of Grace. [56] "Here are some excerpts from eleven of the best-known modern translations; they were by no means all produced by evangelicals, much less by men of Calvinistic persuasion. To avoid any appearance of an attempt to build a case by special ordering, I have simply set them down in alphabetical order. I have also carefully respected the use of capitals by the original authors, a use which can have significance since it sometimes reflects the author's reverence and respect for his subject."

# BAPTIST VOICES IN HISTORY

## ALTERNATIVE RENDERINGS OF ROMANS 8:29

1. An American Translation (Smith and Goodspeed; Chicago: University of Chicago Press, 1923): "For those whom he had *marked out* from the first he predestinated to be made like his Son."

2. The Emphasized Bible (Joseph B. Rotherham; Grand Rapids: Kregel, 1959): "For whom He *foreapproved* He also fore-appointed to be conformed unto the image of His Son."

3. Good News for Modern Man (London; British and Foreign Bible Society, 1966): "For those whom God *had already chosen* he had also set apart to become like his Son."

4. The Holy Bible in Modern English (Ferrar Fenton; London: Black, 1903): "For he *previously knew them*, and appointed them to conformity with the image of his Son."

5. The Jerusalem Bible (ed. Alexander Jones; New York: Doubleday & Co., 1966): "They are the ones he *chose specially long ago* and intended to become true images of his Son."

6. The New English Bible (Oxford University Press and Cambridge, 1970): "For God *knew his own before ever they were*, and also ordained that they should be shaped to the likeness of his Son."

7. The New Testament: A New Translation, Vol. 2 (William Barclay; London: Collins, 1969): "For *long ago, before they ever came into being, God both knew them* and marked them out to become like the pattern of his Son."

8. The New Testament: A New Translation (James

# UNCONDITIONAL ELECTION

Moffatt; New York: Hodder & Stoughton, no date):
"For he *decreed of old* that those whom he predestined should share the likeness of his Son."

9. The New Testament: An Expanded Translation
   (Kenneth S. Wuest; Grand Rapids: Eerdmans, 1961):
   "Because those whom He *foreordained* He also
   marked out beforehand as those who were to be
   conformed to the derived image of His Son."

10. The New Testament: A Translation in the Lan-
    guage of the People (Charles B. Williams; Chicago:
    Moody Press, 1937): "For those *on whom He set
    His heart beforehand* He marked off as His own
    to make like His Son." (A footnote says: "Literally,
    foreknew, but in the LXX used as translated.)

11. The Twentieth Century New Testament (Chicago:
    Moody Bible Institute, 1967): "For those *whom
    God chose from the first* he also did predestinate to
    be conformed to the image of his Son."

**William Williams** also helped in the founding of Southern
Baptist Theological Seminary and later became a professor
there. He had been a professor at Mercer University in Georgia.
Williams stood with Boyce, Broadus, and Manly upon the solid
foundation of God's glorious doctrine of electing grace. [57]

**Basil Manly** was instrumental in the founding of the Southern
Baptists' first seminary, Southern Seminary, in 1859 and was
one of the original four professors on the first faculty. He was
also selected to draw up the "Abstract of Principles". This
confession of faith still endures today and is signed by tenured
Southern Seminary professors. What follows is section V. of

that Abstract, entitled "Election."

"Election is God's eternal choice of some persons
unto everlasting life–not because of foreseen merit in
them, but of his mere mercy in Christ–in consequence
of which choice they are called, justified and glorified."

Manly left Southern Seminary in 1863 to serve as the first
president of the Southern Baptist Sunday School Board, which
had recently formed. Manly was committed to the doctrines of
election. Mueller describes the "Abstract" as a "confessional
statement of the Southern Baptist denomination which they
intended to serve." [58]

**E. C. Dargan**, President of the Southern Baptist Convention
(1911-1913), professor at the Southern Baptist Theological Seminary and at one time editor of the Southern Baptist Sunday
School Board, states in a section that he writes on election–"This
simply means choice–it is divine sovereignty and saving. God's
plan of work for the universe takes in the saving of men. If He
plans to save, He chooses those who will be saved. He will save
those whom He has chosen." [59]

Dargan is quoted in By His Grace and For His Glory as
saying that election is unconditional, "not 'because he foresees
that a man will repent, or on the condition of faith,' but in this
choice God is 'sovereign, free, untrammeled, gracious, acting
on his own initiative.' The same sovereign works in regeneration. The Holy Spirit works in a sovereign way to change the
lives and affections of those whom God has chosen to save.

'What shall we say to these things?', Dargan would ask and
then answer in the spirit of Paul: 'If he chooses some, regener-
ates them, and actually saves them ... we can only answer with
all reverence that this is God's affair, and he will see to it.'" [60]

# UNCONDITIONAL ELECTION

__J. B. Tidwell__ "taught for thirty-six years as head of the Bible Department at Baylor University until his death in 1946. For over twenty years Tidwell's expositions of the Uniform Sunday School lesson appeared in the Texas *Baptist Standard*. " [61]

In his book, By His Grace and For His Glory, Dr. Nettles gives us the doctrinal views of J. B. Tidwell that otherwise would be lost in historical obscurity:

> "'Salvation is the biggest Christian word, and includes first, a plan of salvation, which is all of the Father; second, the preparation of salvation, which was wrought out of Jesus the Son; and third, the application of salvation, which is accomplished by the power of the Holy Spirit. All this involves the great divine covenant of redemption; the work of the atonement of Christ and the regenerating and sanctifying work of the Holy Spirit.'

In answering the question 'What is election?' Tidwell says that 'it is God's decree to act so that certain ones will believe and be saved.' Clearly, by such a decree, God has chosen 'certain men to receive his unmerited grace and be made voluntary recipients of Christ's salvation.' Without such action on God's part, none would receive Jesus; all would reject him. For this reason, eternal election results in an efficacious call, which 'infallibly leads the sinner to salvation.'

Tidwell poses another question: 'When does he elect?' Certainly not after man chooses him, nor is it contemporaneous with man's choice. Election, according to Ephesians 1:4, took place before the foundation of the world. This is the only view that is reasonable and 'makes God sovereign.' What conditions aid or determine God's choice? No merit in those chosen, nor even repentance and faith, serve as conditions. In fact, election is unconditional and rests solely 'in the sovereign will and wisdom of God.' Nor is it on the foreknowledge of our obedience, because our election precedes and brings about obedience. Foreknowledge of merit or holiness falls short also, because we are chosen unto holiness or that we might be holy. Neither is it on foreknowledge of repentance and faith, because these themselves 'are the gifts of God's grace and are the effect of the election rather than its cause.'" [62]

**F. H. Kerfoot**, corresponding secretary of the Home Mission Board and successor to J. P. Boyce as Professor of Theology at Southern Seminary, was so confident that Baptists were Calvinists that he stated, "As we have in common with a large body of evangelical Christians and nearly all Baptists believe what are usually termed 'the doctrines of grace.'" Brother Kerfoot taught:

". . . the absolute sovereignty and foreknowledge of God; his eternal and unchangeable purposes or decrees; that salvation in its beginning, continuance and completion, is God's free gift; that, in Christ, we are elected or chosen, personally, or individually, from eternity, saved and called out from the world, not according to our works, but according to His own purpose and grace, through the sanctification of the Spirit and belief of the truth; that we are kept by His power from falling away, and will be presented faultless before the presence of His glory. Read Romans 8, 9, 10, 11; Acts 13:48; Ephesians 1:4, 5; Ephesians 2:1-10; I Peter 1:2-5; Jude 24; I Timothy 1:9; Titus 3:5." [63]

Dr. Nettles can confidently declare that Kerfoot's "statement is no exaggeration, for up to this time (d. 1904 ca.) no significant Southern Baptist voice had dissented from this view." [64]

**J. B. Gambrell** - As stated on page one, Brother Gambrell was president of the Southern Baptist Convention (1917-1920), one-time editor of the *Baptist Standard*, professor of ecclesiology at Southern Baptist Theological Seminary, editor of the *Baptist Record* in Mississippi, and generally prominent Southern Baptist in the first part of the twentieth century. He was staunch in his views on Unconditional Election and Absolute Predestination. However, he was careful to defend the place of gospel preaching and to show how essential evangelism is in God's plan to call in His elect. He says concerning predestination:

"It is wise in all its goings, selecting and making efficient all means leading to the end. 'If a man is going to be saved he will be saved anyway,' is not true. He will be saved, but God's way, not anyway. And God's way is by the preaching of the gospel, which he has given command shall be preached to every creature. Through the preaching of the gospel he will take out of all nations a people for himself." [65]

Gambrell sums up his position by saying:

"'We glory in the divine sovereignty in predestination, and in the election of grace'—but to imply Hardshellism from those doctrines should be shunned 'as we would the black plague.'" [66]

**W. T. Conner** taught theology at Southwestern Baptist Theological Seminary in Fort Worth for 39 years. He retired from teaching in 1949. His book, <u>Christian Doctrine</u>, in which these few excerpts are found, was published by Broadman Press in

1934.

## "GOD'S PURPOSE AS RELATED TO THE SALVATION OF THE INDIVIDUAL"

### The Meaning of the Doctrine

But the Scriptures teach, not only that God has a general plan that is being carried out in human history, but also that God's purpose applies to the individual. When a man is saved he is not saved as a matter of chance or accident or fate; he is saved in pursuance of an eternal purpose of God. God saves men because he intends to. He saves a particular man, at a particular time, under a given set of circumstances, because he intends to. Election does not mean that God instituted a general plan of salvation and decreed that whosoever would should be saved and therefore the man who wills to be saved is elected in that he brings himself within the scope of God's plan. It is true God has decreed that whosoever will, shall be saved but election is something more specific and personal than that. It means that God has decreed to bring certain ones, upon whom his heart has been eternally set, who are the objects of his eternal love, to faith in Jesus as Saviour. The general meaning of the doctrine of election might be summed up in two statements.

### 1. All Saving Efficiency is of God.

The first is that, when a sinner repents of his sins and believes in Christ to the saving of his soul, he does so because God has brought him to do so. Men do not turn from sin to God on their own initiative. God must move them to do so if ever they turn. This includes all good influences, all gospel agencies, all circumstances of environment, all inner dispositions and promptings of heart and conscience that enter into one's decision. It includes the whole historical order in which one is so situated as to have gospel privileges, and this order is viewed as being providential. Especially does it include the inner promptings and leadings of the Holy Spirit. The gospel of Christ is the gospel of a seeking God. He seeks worshippers (John 4:23). The Son of Man came to seek and to save the lost (Luke 19:10). The seeking of the Son of Man is a revelation of the heart of God. Drawing men to Christ is the work of God. Without this drawing power, men cannot come to Christ (John 6:44).

Paul talks about God as calling men (Romans 8:28-30; I Cor. 1:24, et al.). By this calling he seems to mean more than a general gospel invitation to men to be saved by the grace of God. Paul's use of the term seems to correspond rather to what Jesus speaks of as the drawing of God in John 6:44. It is a dealing of God with the hearts of men that results in their coming to Christ and being saved. This efficacious call does not come to all, not even to all who hear the gospel. Some are called; to them the gospel is the power of God. To others the gospel is a stumbling block or foolishness (I Cor. 1:23). This call gives one a spiritual mind that enables him to get an insight into the meaning of the Cross. The drawing power of God is necessary, because man's natural inclinations are so opposed to God and righteousness that without it man will not come to God. Paul tells us that the carnal mind is enmity against God.

2. God Saves in Pursuance of an Eternal Purpose.
But we must go further back yet. Not only did God

work to bring us to himself; he worked in pursuance of a plan that is eternal. He did not suddenly decide to work for a certain man's salvation; he worked for the man's salvation because he purposed to do so from eternal ages (Romans 8:29, 30; Ephesians 1:4-11; 3:10, 11 et al.). The doctrine of election clearly means that God takes the initiative in our salvation. It means that what he does in saving us he does because he purposed to do it. Our salvation is not a matter of chance nor accident. We are saved because God meant for us to be saved. He saves us and he does so on purpose. He works through the unceasing ages to carry out his purpose. It hardly represents this doctrine fairly to think of it as meaning that God arbitrarily chose this man and this man to be saved and omitted that one and that one. There are depths within the divine counsel that we cannot fathom, of course. But the doctrine does stand for the fact that from all eternity God has had his heart set upon his people for good, and that through the ages he is working out his purpose of grace concerning them (II Timothy 1:9). But there is nothing arbitrary in his actions or purposes. Above all, there is nothing unloving or ungracious in his attitude toward any man." [67]

**Dr. Tom Nettles** has been Chairman of the Church History Department at Mid-America Baptist Theological Seminary in Memphis, Tennessee. Prior to this, Dr. Nettles was Assistant Professor of Church History at Southwestern Baptist Theological Seminary. He states, "Calvinistic soteriology was the sine qua non of the gospel for early Southern Baptists. In fact, that system inhered so naturally within Southern Baptist Life for its first eighty years that a leading denominational statesman of the early twentieth century could say, without fear of contradiction, 'nearly all Baptists believe what are usually termed the "doctrines of grace".'"

Consider these assertions by Dr. Nettles: "The doctrine of unconditional election, perhaps more than any other biblical doctrine, inspires a marvelous awe before the almighty God and humbles his creatures. While shattering all glory that man may seek for himself, the doctrine rivets in our minds the truth that God indeed is the blessed and only potentate, the King of Kings and Lord of Lords who will bring to pass in his own time not only the appearing of our Lord Jesus Christ but all things. To him be honor and might forever!

"In spite of its purpose to give sole glory to God, unconditional election is perhaps one of the most feared and ignored doctrines in contemporary evangelicalism. Many who affirm that God has given man an errorless revelation and who should delight in preaching the whole counsel of God have somehow failed to see the strategic position of this teaching in Scripture.

"In short, the doctrine of election states that—before the foundation of the world—God chose certain individuals to salvation and ordained the means by which they are saved. It is hardly a matter of dispute that this is a very clear teaching of many passages in Scripture.

"Furthermore, if it is revealed and should be believed, election must also be taught and preached. No doctrine of God's Word will ever harm his people. Anyone who believes it dangerous or unwise to teach election is accusing God of a lack of compassion and wisdom, for he alone is the preeminent propagator of the doctrine. The proper teaching of this doctrine is no more dangerous than the proper teaching of the deity of

Christ. Just as errors must be carefully avoided when formulating one's understanding of God's sovereignty in electing grace, so must devastating errors be avoided when setting the deity of Christ in its proper context with the humanity of Christ and his relationship with the Triune God. If a scalpel is deadly, one should not reject its proper life-preserving function.

"In the form of Process Theology, modern theological thinking has finally reached its logical antithesis to the God of Calvinism and the Bible. The god of Process Theology is hardly identifiable as a person, has no power to control history, has only a relative understanding of justice, and knows little more than man does about what is right and wrong in the terribly complex problems that confront us today. Process Theology views history as moving and fluctuating and undulating with no ultimate goal or purpose and, in the process, "god" is being formed. It is, therefore, essentially atheistic.

"That is the only resting place for theology, once the sovereign God of the Bible has been compromised in any way...Once God's sovereignty is diminished for the supposed sake of human freedom, we take a path that will untimately shatter all meaning and justice and leave us not only with no god but with no humanity. When this happens, there is also no gospel, no true Christian mission, no holiness to pursue, no standard to which we are to be conformed."[68]

# UNCONDITIONAL ELECTION

### *Invitation Accepted*

1. *Am I called? and can it be!*
   *Has my Saviour chosen me?*
   *Guilty, wretched, as I am,*
   *Has he named my worthless name?*
   *Vilest of the vile am I;*
   *Dare I raise my hopes so high?*

2. *Am I called?  I dare not stay;*
   *May not, must not, disobey;*
   *Here I lay me at thy feet,*
   *Clinging to the mercy-seat:*
   *Thine I am, and thine alone;*
   *Lord, with me thy will be done.*

3. *Am I called?  What shall I bring*
   *As an offering to my King?*
   *Poor, and blind, and naked, I*
   *Trembling at thy footstool lie:*
   *Nought but sin I call my own;*
   *Nor for sin can sin atone.*

4. *Am I called?—an heir of God!*
   *Washed, redeemed, by precious blood!*
   *Father, lead me in thy hand,*
   *Guide me to that better land,*
   *Where my soul shall be at rest,*
   *Pillowed on my Saviour's breast.*

*HYMN TUNES:  Gethsemane, Dix, Toplady*

*Sample hymn from the days of our SBC forefathers* [88]

# Salvation By Grace Through Faith

The truth of Unconditional Election has direct application to personal salvation, in that only those whom God has chosen to be saved will be saved. This seems to be a hard pill to swallow. The voices of earth cry out "unfair!" or, "that reduces man to a robot!" or, "God would not be so cruel!" <u>Our minds quickly think of myriads of people who want to be saved and yet cannot be if God makes the decision regarding who will be and who won't be.</u> Possibly a Bible teacher has cast the doctrine of election in such a scenario showing God as forcing some to be saved who do not want to be–kicking and screaming all the way. Many others are seen as wanting to be saved but are turned away because of some arbitrary selection process whereby they were not "lucky" enough to be selected. These are unfair and unwarranted caricatures of God's sovereign love and mercy. Only man's wicked pride and prejudiced confusion can account for such ludicrous imaginations. Every Christian, as our Baptist forefathers did, ought to be able to read any of the scripture texts that explicitly state God's sovereign purpose of election as applied to salvation, and rejoice with praise.

## A Bad Record

Most evangelicals understand quite well that man, apart from Christ, is legally guilty and condemned because of personal sin (Romans 3:9, 19) and is presently under the wrath of God (John 3:36) with the threat of eternal vengeance looming over his head (Romans 2:5; I Thess. 1:8, 9). Man is a lawbreaker.

81

# UNCONDITIONAL ELECTION

He finds himself condemned before the Eternal Judge of all the earth. Man's only hope is the justification freely offered in the gospel which can be appropriated by faith alone apart from the works of the law (Romans 3:21-31; Galatians 2:16). A gracious God, the Father of our Lord Jesus Christ, has provided a righteousness through His Son, which not only wipes our bad record of offences and transgressions clean, but also imputes to us a perfect obedience to the whole law of God. We are made "right with God!" We are made fit for heaven to live forever in His presence! No longer is hell a threat for a blood-washed child of God. We are justified freely and stand before the Judge with perfect righteousness on our record. Legally we are as righteous as God Himself. All this is through our substitute Lamb–the righteous Son of God–Jesus Christ. His atoning work at Calvary has paid the sin debt. What wondrous love is this!

## A Bad Heart

Man's problem is nevertheless much greater than just a legal one. There is more to his dilemma than transgressions, guilt, wrath, condemnation, and hell. A great many evangelicals at this point do not seem to realize the extent of man's depravity. Man has a heart problem–a sinful and corrupt nature that governs his mind, affections, and will. Just one glance at the Great Physician's report reveals a startling diagnosis.

Every human being by nature is spiritually:

1. Dead - Ephesians 2:1; Romans 5:12
2. Blind - Ephesians 4:18
3. Defiled in conscience - Titus 1:15, 16
4. Trapped in darkness - Colossians 1:13
5. Without understanding - I Corinthians 2:14
6. Enslaved in sin - John 8:34

7.  Hostile toward God - Romans 8:7
8.  A hater of the light - John 3:19, 20
9.  Without desire for God - Romans 3:11
10. Without fear of God - Romans 3:18

If just one of these descriptions is true, man is in deep trouble. But to man's utter woe and misery, all of these gruesome descriptions are true. Man, by nature, operates with a heart that is totally devoid of God, of God's presence, of God's favor, of God's righteousness, of God's graces. Man has no saving understanding of God, no saving affections for God, and no saving faith in God. He does not possess any of these qualities in himself. Try as he may to know God, and relate to God, man is both *incapable* of and *uninterested* in coming to the God of the Bible on His terms.

## Spiritually Dead

How dead is dead? A redundant question? Not according to many who suggest man has a spark of life within, at least enough spiritual life to make his own decision for Christ. Jesus talked in terms of stone-cold corpses, tombs, and resurrections. Lazarus did not initiate his dealings with Christ, nor did he exercise a "free will" to come to life. Ezekiel's dry bones did not rattle with consent under the prophet's ministry. Is it any wonder that Jesus said, "No man can come to me" in John 6:44, 65 in relation to their need of the Bread of Life? In Adam all are dead (Romans 5:12-21; I Corinthians 15:22)! How can a dead man have understanding, affections, or a will in the realm to which he is dead?

## Without Understanding

Remember the last time you tried to explain something to a

child, and it obviously did not "click" in his mind? Better yet, remember the joke or riddle someone told you and you did not "get it?" Recently a dear friend of mine suffered a slight blow to the head which resulted in severe amnesia. Attempts to relate even in the most simple terms were frustrating for both our friend and others.

Jesus has described man's condition as "without under-standing." Man is in the dark. Spiritual things do not "register" in the spiritual mind of the natural man. He cannot see. He cannot hear. He cannot discern. He cannot understand. These scriptures make this clear: I Corinthians 2:10-14; Ephesians 4:18; II Corinthians 4:4; Romans 1:21, 22; Titus 1:15; Matthew 11:25, 13:10-16; John 8:43, 47; Acts 26:18. Man may stack up Bible studies, Bible knowledge, Bible meetings, ad infinitum, and yet never receive spiritual understanding—the inner light of God's Spirit—that brings a saving apprehension of his sinful misery, a saving fear of God, a saving hope in Christ, a saving devotion to the glory of God. Make no mistake, the preaching of the Gospel, careful Bible studies, and witnessing conversa-tions are the very means God uses to bring salvation—the light of life. But they in themselves will mean nothing spiritually to an otherwise dead, blind, deaf, darkened, biased spiritual mind.

## Hostile Toward God

When Paul stated in Romans 8:7, "The carnal mind is enmity against God, for it is not subject to the law of God nor indeed can be," he spoke in agreement with Jesus, who said that the people of this world hate Him and His Father (John 7:7, 15:23). Jesus also informed us of man's natural hatred for the purity and revelation of God—John 3:19, 20—and man will not come to it. Man, by nature, wants no part of a God of holiness.

# SALVATION BY GRACE THROUGH FAITH

All men are as sheep going astray, going their own way, and refuse to have this man–Jesus–to rule over them. There is no desire in man for God. There is no fear of God in man whatsoever. Perhaps he has some superstitious, slavish fear, but nothing of a saving, reverential fear producing a desire to honor God as God and to walk humbly in His ways with a due sense of exalting God for His incomparable glory. Man despises God as revealed in the Scriptures. He refuses to worship Him and love Him in spirit and in truth. He refuses to submit daily to God's word and to obey Christ out of a heart of love and gratitude. Man's natural bent is to fight God, oppose God, and run from God. To speak of the unsaved as hungering and thirsting for God is to contradict Scripture. They may hunger and thirst for something–and they do–but never is it for the God of Heaven in their natural condition. They may seek God for their selfish ends–for His eternal benefits and blessings, but never does the natural man desire to seek or love a holy God in devotion to Him and His glory. It is relatively easy to chalk up "decisions" for Christ by parading the goodies of safety and happiness before the natural man, but a reformed sinner is still a lost sinner–hostile toward God as revealed in His holiness, His commandments, and His holy will.

## Man's Nature and Will

This is man's nature: *Incapable* of coming to God on His terms and *uninterested* in doing so, even if he could. Man is enslaved by sin (John 8:34), governed by his sinful lusts (Ephesians 2:3), controlled by this world's system (Ephesians 2:2), and captive to the devil (Ephesians 2:2). A careful study of Ephesians 2:1-3 will produce no other honest conclusion. Man is helplessly, hopelessly bound to his own sinful tyranny and is

85

ruled continually by the dictates of his fleshly lusts.

Man will not choose God, nor His Son, Jesus Christ on *real gospel terms*. Man cannot choose Christ the Lord because he is so ruined by the fall. That is why Jesus taught, "No man can come to me" (John 6:44, 65)–"he cannot see the kingdom of God" (John 3:3)–"You are not able to listen to my word" (John 8:47)–"You do not believe because you are not of my sheep" (John 10:26).

The spiritual understanding, affections, and will of man are dead, bound, biased, and rebellious. These are the kind of sinners the church is seeking to bring to Christ. Could there be any more impossible task than holding the light of the lovely Lord Jesus before such unholy, unreceptive mortals as these? If any one of them shall be saved, it will be wholly of God's power. Man indeed has a serious heart problem, more so than most have realized.

**Free Will**

As the Bible teaches Unconditional Election, man's natural response is,"What about free will?–we all have free will, don't we?" It seems as though this concern about free will inevitably becomes the central focus in the whole discussion about election. The Baptist Faith and Message states on page 12 that election is "consistent with the free agency of man." This does not mean, however, that man's will is sovereign and so powerful as to cast the ultimate and deciding vote as to whether he will be saved or not.

May I hasten to say that man is a creature of choice and has been divinely endowed with a will–a chooser–this is a given. Folks all through the Bible chose to obey God or not to obey God–to receive Jesus or not to receive Him. As we preach and witness to the lost, we appeal, not only to the understanding and affections of men, but also to their wills. We press them to bow to God's word. We warn them that they must flee to Christ for refuge. We encourage them to "decide" to eat and drink of our Savior. They must call upon Him for salvation, and that means they must decide to do it. In this sense, man is a free agent. However, He chooses to do what he *wants* to do. The key problem with man is not his faculty of choice, but his disposition of heart to *desire*. In other words, man left to himself *will not* choose salvation through Christ on God's terms. Not only is the natural man dead and darkened spiritually, but he is hostile–biased against Christ's righteous rule and holy ways. No matter how we candy-coat the Gospel with sugary hope and happiness, or arm it with Sinai's heaviest threats of judgment, sinners will not want Jesus as He is offered in the Gospel. Therefore, man's will is not so free after all. A brief word study on the word "can" will speak to man's ability or inability to come to Christ. Key verses to include in such a study would be John 3:3-8; 5:40-44; 6:44, 65; 8:43-47; Matthew 19:25, 26; Romans 8:7, 8; I Corinthians 2:14. These verses say that man cannot–he is not free. Again, he is responsible to believe unto salvation, but God's word says that man is *not able* because he is *incapable* and *uninterested*.

This thorny issue became highlighted in the Protestant Reformation. Martin Luther brought the church back to an emphatic stand on justification by faith, and faith alone, apart from the works of the Law. However, the core issue of Luther's reformation was the extent of man's depravity and the implications of his entirely corrupted nature. A struggle over this doctrine with the famous Erasmus resulted in Luther's work, The Bondage of the Will. He concluded that man has no saving faith in and of himself by which he may be justified. Man is so bound by sin and darkness and so captivated to the inward lusts and to the devil, that he does not possess one ounce of the faith that brings justification. Man's nature governs his will. He will choose to follow his nature's dictates every time.

In a sample of C. H. Spurgeon's preaching, we see how Spurgeon developed the two truths of man's duty and his sinful inability. Iain Murray describes Spurgeon's use of them as "two jaws of a vice grip upon the sinner's conscience."

"God asks you to believe that through the blood of Jesus Christ, He can still be just, and yet the justifier of the ungodly. He asks you to trust in Christ to save you. Can you expect that He will save you if you will not trust Him? Man, it is the most reasonable thing in the world that He should demand of thee that thou shouldst believe in Christ. And this He does demand of thee this morning. 'Repent and believe the gospel.' O friends, O friends, how sad, how sad is the state of man's soul when he will not do this! We may preach to you, but you never will repent and believe the gospel. We may lay God's commands, like an axe, to the root of the tree, but, reasonable as these commands are, you will still refuse to give God His due; you will go on in your sins; you will not come unto Him that you may have life; and it is here the Spirit of God must come in to work in the souls of the elect to make them willing in the day of His power. But oh! in God's name I warn you that, if, after hearing this command, you do, as I know you will do, without His Spirit, continue to refuse obedience to so reasonable a gospel, you shall find at the last it shall be more tolerable for Sodom and Gomorrah, than for you; for had the things which are preached in London been proclaimed in Sodom and Gomorrah, they would have repented long ago in sackcloth and in ashes. Woe unto you, inhabitants of London!" [69]

**Gift of Free Will**

Some who confess man's "total" depravity are led to conclude that God has at some point in time *superimposed* upon man an ability–a free will–to make an unbiased, uncoerced decision for Christ upon hearing the gospel. They are sure God must have done this because of the issue of fairness and man's dignity (i.e., robots, etc.). After all, man is expected to repent and believe as continually stated in scripture. Therefore, if man is expected to respond, God must have bestowed the ability to man of "free choice." But I ask you, dear reader, do you know of one scripture that verifies this idea? Can you refer to one verse that verifies this superimposing of a neutral ability? Do you not find yourself going back to verses that say God calls for man to choose, to decide, to call, to believe? But nowhere can this superimposed capacity within man to have sovereign freedom of choice be supported by Holy Scripture. Man is duty bound, yet sin bound.

**Foreseen Faith**

Maybe you have explained election and predestination before in this way: "Before the world began God looked into the future, foresaw who would choose Him and then elected those individuals based only on their free choice of Him." This explanation has been the classic Arminian approach through the centuries. It seeks to reconcile God's election with man's freedom. There are several problems with this position.

# UNCONDITIONAL ELECTION

First, it fails to appreciate the utter ruin that man has fallen into. It suggests man is not quite dead, not completely without understanding, and not fully hostile against God. It sets man up as having the possibility within himself of desiring righteousness, of understanding his need in light of God's truth, and of making a change of his own mind toward God–from hostility to endearment.

Secondly, this position is a direct denial of what clear scripture teaches. What did God see when He looked into the future at fallen man? He saw sheep going astray, turning every one to his own way! The Psalmist answers the question concerning what God foresaw when He looked at man:

"The Lord looks down from heaven on the sons of men to see if there are any who understand, any who seek God. All have turned aside, they have together become corrupt; there is no one who does good, not even one."
Psalm 14:2,3

Paul writes the exact same conclusion with regard to what God saw–Romans 3:10-18! There is not one verse of scripture indicating that God saw us choosing Him of our own volition.

Thirdly, the scriptures used to prove this position–Romans 8:29; 11:2; I Peter 1:2–are not given with accurate exegesis. This position of foreseen faith is forced on the texts. The thing foreknown in Romans 8:29 is not an "it," but rather a "who". These scriptures do not speak of what God could see, but of whom God "knew" (had intimate regard for, loved). For more discussion on the words "foreknew, foreknowledge" see the section on B. H. Carroll in Chapter 2.

## Unfair !

How often it has been said, "If God elects individuals of His own choosing, without their having any say in the matter, and if others who are not chosen cannot be saved–that's unfair!" However, it all depends upon which standard of "fairness" we are using. No wonder the Scripture says "the natural mind does not receive the things of the Spirit of God (I Corinthians 2:14)"! Election is <u>unconditional</u>–that is, there is <u>nothing</u> in the sinner that moved God to choose him–and it is <u>absolutely sovereign</u>–that is, God was freely directed in whom He chose only by the good pleasure of His own will. In other words, He elected unto salvation only those individuals whom He wanted to elect (Ephesians 1:4-6, 9, 11; II Timothy 1:9). If this seems "unfair" to you, please consider four factors.

First, if God were to be "fair," or to give us what we justly deserve, we would be in a "world of hurt," literally. I don't know about you, but I would not want God to be fair with me as I stand apart from His Son. Remember, God owes us nothing but hell itself.

In the second place, it is not as though those who are not elected are beating down the door of salvation wanting the Lord Jesus to rule over them. None of them, in themselves, want the salvation of Jesus Christ anyway.

Thirdly, we are assured that anyone who comes to Christ in faith is received (John 6:37). He will cast none out. He will reject none. Let them come! The offer goes to all. Let them come and they will be graciously received, if, of course, they come on real gospel terms.

Lastly, Paul anticipated this very objection–God being "unfair" –in Romans 9:14 ff., and gave the inspired response. He says, "No! God is not unfair nor unrighteous. He can do with wicked, hell-deserving sinners as He sees fit, and He will! He will show mercy and compassion to whomever He is pleased to show it, and it has nothing to do with man's efforts or will in the matter." He is God and He unapologetically exercises His divine right of sovereignty! You see, dear friend, God decides what is fair. He may operate on a standard of fairness that our sinful, finite minds cannot grasp, but He will do it anyway, because He is the righteous God. If this seems unloving to the human mind, please put it in perspective. Who has turned against whom? Who has blasphemed whom? Who has gone off in rebellion, debauchery, and self-will? Who is the Potter and who is the clay? Who has created whom? Who has issued centuries of loving addresses to whom and sent prophets, worked miracles, given written revelation, sustained life by food, water, climate, shelter, etc., etc.? Who was it that sent His only and Eternal Son to pay a gruesome, yet just penalty for sin? Who now sweetly calls any sinner to come unto Him for rest, for mercy, for salvation? Can this God not do with rebellious mortals as He sees fit? If He were to cast every single human being into an eternal hell fire, would He be any less just or loving? No! No! No! We must grasp more fully the extent of man's wickedness, rebellion, and just desert of God's wrath. We must grasp more fully God's glorious sovereignty. He alone sits enthroned in heaven's majesty. May every man who speaks of our Sovereign as "unfair" be brought low before his Maker to worship and honor Him with reverence and godly fear.

## Robots?

It is said often that Unconditional Election would reduce men to mere "robots." If man doesn't have the ultimate power of choice to determine his own destiny, how can he be held responsible for his actions? Paul anticipated this objection as well, in Romans 9:19. See Paul's response in verse 20, 21:

## SALVATION BY GRACE THROUGH FAITH

"You will say to me, then, 'Why does He still find fault? For who has resisted His will?' But indeed, O man, who are you to reply against God? Will the thing formed say to him who formed it, 'Why have you made me like this?' Does not the potter have power over the clay, from the same lump to make one vessel for honor, and another for dishonor?"

God is God! He has His purpose and will carry it out. Dr. Samuel Storms put it this way in his book, Chosen For Life:

"God has the undisputed right to give full and artistic display to all his attributes and skills as a craftsman by making vessels as he sees fit, either for honorable use or common use. The creature has no more of a right to pro-test how God dispenses with creation than does a piece of clay have a right to dictate instructions to the potter. To be perfectly blunt about it, God can do what he jolly well pleases to do, with or without our approval!" [70]

Let me also say that Unconditional Election does not reduce men to robots in view of the fact that God operates in the whole of the human personality when saving a person. He deals with the understanding, the affections, and the will. *He never forces a person to be saved against his will*. He does what He has to do if any person will ever be saved–He changes the man's heart. Consequently his whole personality complies, including the will.

### Why?

Why has God chosen to save some specific individuals and leave others in their own heart's condition to have what they prefer? Paul tells us in Romans 9:22, 23. He will display His mighty power (vv. 22, 17) and the richness of His glorious mercy

# UNCONDITIONAL ELECTION

(v. 23). This agrees with what Paul said in Ephesians 1:6, 12, 14 and in 2:7. God has done it all for Himself. His glorious grace and mercy will be displayed all over the heavens and the earth for the praise of His name! Does this sound selfish and egotistical to you? Remember, you are mere clay in the hand of a sovereign Potter!

## Salvation by Grace

Grace speaks of blessing bestowed to the undeserving, to the unqualified. Grace is magnified when we realize man is not only "undeserving," but "ill-deserving." Our sin is such that we are justly said to be objects of God's wrath prior to conversion–John 3:36; Romans 1:18; 2:5; Ephesians 2:3.

Grace points away from the recipient to the Giver as to why the blessing should be bestowed. Grace is set in opposition to work or merit–Romans 11:5, 6. We are justified freely by His grace–Romans 3:24. Any works or merit in man makes the bestowed blessing a matter of debt; therefore grace has nothing to do with what the sinner performs. Dead people do not cooperate. If man is merely sick, he can cooperate with the Physician's instructions to get well. But a dead man cannot. We must think Grace. Our faith, which is not our faith at all, does not trigger God's grace. God's grace bestows faith to us simply because of the sovereign goodness of the Donor.

If God's grace is not seen in light of Unconditional Election, salvation is no longer all of grace. God's grace is not dependent upon any conditions that man can meet. The very faith that God requires of man, He sovereignly bestows.

Allow me to share a progression of ideas that I believe define and magnify God's grace.

1.   There is no worth in man to deserve God's favor.

2. There is nothing in man but unworthiness.
3. All that is in man deserves anything but favor.
4. Grace subdues man in spite of all his abuses to God's favor and mercy.
5. Grace not only forgives, but condescends to draw into a most intimate union, relationship, fellowship, and honor.
6. Grace is bestowed at an extraordinary cost to purchase all that it means to give.

Understanding God's grace should humble us and change the emphasis of our testimonies. Instead of saying, "I turned," "I repented," "I believed," or "I became a Christian," we should be found marveling at God's sovereign, overcoming grace by saying, "God saved me," "God had mercy to change my heart," and "God gave me faith to believe, eyes to see, ears to hear, and a heart to believe." Our emphasis will be like Paul's when grace is properly seen (I Timothy 1:13, 14; Ephesians 2:4-7).

### How God Does It–Regeneration

How does God begin to transform mortals who are spiritually dead, bound by sin, defiled, biased, haters of God? By nature they oppose God and will never bow to Him, believe in Him, or apply to Him for saving grace.

He does something very powerful called "quickening" (Ephesians 2:5). This "regeneration" is the infusing of life into the soul where death has reigned. The "new birth" is an act of God. The new birth produces the effects of repentance and faith. Arminian theology turns that around to say a man's faith produces the new birth. This again fails to appreciate man's heart problem for the total ruin and utter impotence that is there. You hear it illustrated during altar calls especially, when sinners are instructed to come forward, pray a prayer, and receive the new birth; they will be born again. They are put in control of salvation. They can do something to effect their change of heart.

This is exactly opposite to our Lord's teaching to Nicodemus in John 3. Jesus told Nicodemus of the way of the new birth as applied to the heart. In verse 8, the Holy Spirit's blowing of life into a soul is compared to the wind. You cannot tell where it comes from or where it is going. It blows where it wants to. So is everyone who is born of the Spirit. The Spirit blows *where He wants to*. As the Spirit of Christ, He quickens whomever He will–John 5:21. He is a sovereign dispenser of life to the soul, and man cannot effect that blowing by going through three or four mechanical steps. It is in this way that God opened Lydia's heart to the gospel message (Acts 16:14). God did not disregard Lydia's will–He changed her heart in such a way that she began to choose the things of God in a life of faith and obedience. The new birth is not accomplished by the will of man deciding it will happen–John 1:13; Romans 9:16–but because God decides to save a particular man at a particular time. There is nothing man can do or will do to effect his new birth.

The Baptist Faith and Message declares saving faith to be a response to the regenerating work of the Holy Spirit. Baptists used to believe that regeneration caused faith and not vice versa. Arminian theology had to place faith as a cause of regeneration because, logically, if a person were made regenerate before conversion, could he then decide not to be converted? Arminians couldn't live with that. They demand that man's will dish out the instructions rather than consent to God's grace sovereignly changing the heart.

Another aspect of irresisible grace is effectual calling. It is the sovereign work in the heart that guarantees justification

(Romans 8:30). Note in this verse that every person who is called, *without exception*, is justified. Not one refuses the offer or rejects the Lord.

Notice, as well, that God's Spirit does not just influence or appeal to them for a while and then turn them over to their wills for a final decision. Everyone who is called with this regenerating, effectual call is made righteous. Some have suggested this idea from John 6:44—that God "draws" in the sense of wooing or enticing a person just so far and then He turns him over to his own will for a final decision to accept or reject. R. C. Sproul speaks to this interpretation:

"Earlier in chapter 6 of John's Gospel Jesus makes a similar statement. He says, 'No one can come to Me unless the Father who sent Me draws him'(John 6:44). The key word here is *draw*. What does it mean for the Father to draw people to Christ? I have often heard this text explained to mean that the Father must woo or entice men to Christ. Unless this wooing takes place, no man will come to Christ. However, man has the ability to resist this wooing and to refuse the enticement. The wooing, though it is necessary, is not compelling. In philosophical language that would mean that the drawing of God is a necessary condition but not a sufficient condition to bring men to Christ. In simpler language it means that we cannot come to Christ without the wooing, but the wooing does not guarantee that we will, in fact, come to Christ.

"I am persuaded that the above explanation, which is so widespread, is incorrect. It does violence to the text of Scripture, particularly to the biblical meaning of the word *draw*. The Greek word used here is *elko*. <u>Kittel's</u>

Theological Dictionary of the New Testament defines it to mean to compel by irresistible superiority. Linguistically and lexicographically, the word means "to compel."

"To compel is a much more forceful concept than to woo. To see this more clearly, let us look for a moment at two other passages in the New Testament where the same Greek word is used. In James 2:6 we read: 'But you have dishonored the poor man. Do not the rich oppress you and *drag* you into the courts?' Guess which word in this passage is the same Greek word that elsewhere is translated by the English word *draw*. It is the word *drag*. Let us now substitute the word *woo* in the text. It would then read: 'Do not the rich oppress you and *woo* you into the courts?'

"The same word occurs in Acts 16:19. 'But when her masters saw that their hope of profit was gone, they seized Paul and Silas and *dragged* them into the marketplace to the authorities.' Again, try substituting the word *woo* for the word drag. Paul and Silas were not seized and then *wooed* into the marketplace." [71]

This internal call, that brings a guaranteed conversion, is not to be confused with the external call set forth in the Scriptures. The external call is the gospel preached to all men, every creature in this earth, to repent of sin and believe in Christ. This call is external only and can be rejected (Matthew 11:28; 28:19; Acts 17:30; Revelation 22:17). This external call is seen clearly in Matthew 22:14: "For many are called, but few are chosen."

The following verses also teach that God is sovereign with regard to who comes to life in Christ: Matthew 11:25-27; John

98

# SALVATION BY GRACE THROUGH FAITH

5:21; James 1:18–"of His own will He brought us forth (begat) by the word of truth."

## Faith

Grace is free and undeserved mercy toward us. Faith is the humble trust with which we receive it to ourselves. Faith is the instrument by which a sinner avails himself of salvation. Faith "turns to and embraces Christ." J. P. Boyce describes the nature of saving faith in five ways:

1. As looking to Christ - Isaiah 45:22; John 3:14-16
2. As coming to Him - Isaiah 55:1-3, 6; Matthew 11:28; John 6:37
3. As eating and drinking Him - John 6:51-58
4. As fleeing to Him and laying hold of Him - Hebrews 6:18
5. As receiving Him - Colossians 2:6 [72]

Tom Wells, in his book, Faith: The Gift of God, observes that faith has three essential elements–understanding, belief, and trust. First, understanding–Do I understand that Jesus Christ is the Eternal God come in the flesh? Do I understand that He has come to save sinners? Do I understand that there is no salvation apart from Him? Do I have eyes to see and ears to hear what these statements mean? Second, belief–Do I believe these statements are true? Have I been convinced in my heart that these claims are exactly right? Thirdly, trust–Do I want Him as revealed in the Word of God as my own Prophet, Priest, and King to apply His salvation to my soul? Do I count Him as trustworthy, and am I disposed to flee to Him with the trust of my eternal soul? [73]

You see, faith is not merely mental assent. Faith is not merely asking Him to give you something that will make you happy and secure. Faith is not adding Jesus to your otherwise established life. Faith is <u>understanding</u> the essential facts and terms of the gospel, <u>believing</u> they are completely true and the precise answer to your need, and <u>applying</u> yourself in a total sense to <u>rely upon</u> and *comply with* the truths and terms of the gospel.

Man does not have this kind of faith. As stated before, man in his natural condition does not understand spiritual things. He does not see or hear them with the eyes or ears of the soul. He does not believe the truths and terms of the Gospel are precisely what he, himself, personally needs, nor is there one particle of inclination to come to Christ in a saving faith and trust. His hostility and inward bias against God are going to manifest their fruits in some way or another, either in an outright fashion or in a more clever, pharisaic or pseudo-Christian approach. But until God implants faith, saving faith, in the soul, there is no genuine conversion. God does this only in His elect.

## Repentance

The very word *repent*, in many minds, strikes up antiquated ideas of some half-goofy charlatan peddling a miracle potion in a traveling medicine show. Hollywood has taken great pains to create negative, even repulsive, sensations in our minds at the very mention of words such as sin, repent, holiness, etc. This has affected the twentieth century pulpit more than we realize. It is not fashionable to speak in such terms. The modern mind recoils in disgust—even the church mind.

Nevertheless, our Lord used the word *repent* as the cutting edge for His gospel preaching (Matthew 4:17; Mark 1:14, 15; Luke 24:47). His disciples followed His example—Mark 6:12. A word study on the word *repent* will produce undeniable evi-

# SALVATION BY GRACE THROUGH FAITH

dence for the vital, essential nature of this truth, especially in the book of Acts, our manual on evangelism.

The Baptist Faith and Message clearly places repentance as a *response* to the sovereign work of regeneration in the heart. This means repentance is intimately linked to election. The man who genuinely repents by the change of heart wrought by the Holy Spirit has been *granted* that repentance from a sovereign God (Acts 11:18; 5:31). God decides when a particular man at a particular time will repent (II Timothy 2:25). It is not within man's power or prerogative to arise from the dead, break the chains that bind him and begin following Christ. Until a sovereign God breaks the death grip of darling sins upon a man's heart, his own lusts and pride will prevent him from pursuing a holy life of pleasing God.

A children's catechism rightly defines repentance as *to be sorry for sin, and to hate and forsake it because it is displeasing to God* (see footnote #40). Bible repentance, then, involves several key elements. In the first place, sin must be understood. The only real place to start in defining sin is in the law of God (I John 3:4). The only true criterion for understanding God's righteousness and any departure from that righteousness is the law of God. The testimony of any true Christian includes the confession of having been dead in trespasses and sins. Men need to know how they have fallen short of the glory of God. They need to know why they are guilty, why they are defiled, and why they are miserable. Many pulpits do not preach God's law, and have made their own laws of holiness. The Ten Commandments are very seldom preached and God's righteousness seldom slays the heart. Jesus took the law and went for the heart of professing converts (The Sermon on the Mount).

Secondly, repentance involves regret. This sorrow of soul

or sense of "being sorry" results when a person sees his sin as an offence to God. His sin displeases God. This man is not regretting sin primarily because it has destroyed his life, or because it has ruined his reputation, or because he could have been so much more productive or happy if he had not chosen a course of sin. His greatest sorrow and regret is that he has offended his Creator, Sustainer, Benefactor, and Judge. Today's pulpits seldom show a sinner's sin in this light.

Again, God's law is the means to effect such remorse. God's law is His broom to stir up the dirt of sin in the soul and to cause a choking effect of sorrow, regret, and shame against the backdrop of God's glorious holiness. If this emphasis is not present in a person professing faith in Christ, he will be a likely candidate to be a hearer described in the Parable of the Sower— a stony-ground hearer, or a thorny-ground hearer, who is not a Christian at all. Paul's experience with God's law should be enough to convince us of the law's irreplaceable contribution in bringing about a deep, heartfelt conviction of sin that leads to a genuine life-changing repentance (Romans 7:7-13).

Thirdly, true repentance always involves an inward disposition to flee to Christ Jesus for mercy. Pardon flows deep and wide in Jesus and the sinner made alive in Christ will be found prostrate at Calvary trusting in nothing but the blood to wash away sin. Judas and Peter both grieved deeply over heinous sin. Only Peter saw mercy in Christ. In preaching the law of God, a true minister will be anxious to point a pain-riven conscience to Golgotha for the healing stream. In one dynamic motion, a sinner turns from sin and casts himself upon Jesus in saving trust.

Fourthly, Bible repentance always continues, accompanied by deep regret for sins in the past, fully determined to avoid sin and obey God. His changed heart cries out against sin and longs for holiness. With a full purpose and new obedience, a man born of the Spirit will not practice sin in his life (I John 3:9). The times that he falls in sin, he will sooner or later agonize as Paul did—"O wretched man that I am!" (Romans 7:24)—yet with that holy principle of God's grace in the soul, he will not lie there and enjoy his sin as in the past. He is God's child; therefore, he will get up, repent, and obey God!

The Apostle John described those truly born of the Spirit as those: 1) who do not make a practice of sin (I John 3:9); and 2) who find their practice and great delight in God's commandments (I John 3:7, 10; 5:1-5). Make no mistake—all the church members of the Southern Baptist Convention or of any other church who show no evangelical obedience to Jesus Christ can have no Bible assurance at all that they are Christians. God's people *will* follow Jesus in obedience and faith (John 10:27).

### How Do I Know Whether or Not I Have Been Elected?

The simple answer to this question is this—In the same way you determine whether you are a Christian or not. Only a person who is grasping for cop-outs to avoid repentance and saving faith will seek to determine his elect status before fleeing to Christ. If a person can, with Biblical support, draw assurance that he is truly born of God, he will have settled the question of whether he has been elected to salvation before the world was.

The Bible way for a person to draw assurance that he has been saved is through self-examining questions—Do I love God more for who He is than for how He makes me happy? Do I love to read the Scriptures? Do I delight in the commandments of God? Is my soul comforted by God's truth? Do I feel real conviction for my sin? Is my life marked by the ongoing pursuit of holiness? Is there a real distinction between myself and the world? Do I love to be with the brethren? Is the worship of God a priority in my life? Does sin grieve me because it grieves God? Is there a willingness to deny self for the glory of God and to serve Christ sacrificially? Is my soul found breathing regularly in secret prayer? Do I make it my life practice to carefully obey God's Word?

These are distinguishing traits of true Christian character. Searching the life for such signs of saving grace is the only Bible way of establishing assurance of salvation. Unlike today's methods, the Bible never teaches us to look to an experience of walking an aisle or of making a salvation decision as grounds for assurance.

How many will plunge into eternal death assuming all is well, fully assured of salvation, because of faith in a one-time decision! Salvation comes at once–assurance is not so instantaneous. Thus we find the admonition in II Peter 1:10: "Therefore, brethren, be even more diligent to make your calling and election sure, for if you do these things you will never stumble."

How can I be assured that I am God's elect? God's redeemed child? By adding these to my faith: virtue, knowledge, self-control, perserverance, godliness, brotherly kindness, and love. This is the only way I can truly know and have assurance that I am a Christian–by growing in the sanctifying graces of God's Spirit (II Peter 1:5-11).

C. H. Spurgeon, in his sermon entitled "Election", gave some thoughts that may help:

"But there are some who say, 'It is hard for God to choose some and leave others.' Now, I will ask you one question. Is there any one of you here this morning who wishes to be holy, who wishes to be regenerate, to leave off sin and walk in holiness? 'Yes, there is,' says some one, 'I do.' Then God has elected you. But another says, 'No: I don't want to be holy; I don't want to give up my lusts and my vices.' Why should you grumble, then, that God has not elected you to it? For if you were elected you would not like it, according to your own confession. If God, this morning, had chosen you to holiness, you say you would not care for it.

Do you not acknowledge that you prefer drunkenness to sobriety, dishonesty to honesty? You love this world's pleasures better than religion; then why should you grumble that God has not chosen you to religion. If you love religion, he has chosen you to it. If you desire it, he has chosen you to it. If you do not, what right have you to say that God ought to have given you what you do not wish for?" [74]

Do you love Christ, holiness, Scripture, obedience, the brethren, prayer, growing in grace, the cross, and the glory of God (though not perfectly, by any means)? Then you are God's

### Regeneration
*John 1:13, 3:3 &c.*

1. Not  all the outward forms on earth,
   Nor rites that God has given,
   Nor will of man, nor blood, nor birth,
   Can raise a soul to heaven.

2. The sovereign will of God alone
   Creates us heirs of grace;
   Born in the image of his Son,
   A new, peculiar race.

3. The Spirit, like some heavenly wind,
   Blows on the sons of flesh;
   New models all the carnal mind,
   And forms the man afresh.

4. Our quickened souls awake, and rise
   From the long sleep of death;
   On heavenly things we fix our eyes,
   And praise employs our breath.

HYMN TUNE: Carol

*Sample hymn from the days of our SBC forefathers* [88]

# WHY THE DOCTRINE OF ELECTION IS ESSENTIAL IN OUR CHURCHES TODAY

( WORSHIP )

Jesus taught the Samaritan woman of John 4 that *true* worship is carried on in *spirit* and in *truth*. He said it *must* be done with a right heart and with right doctrine, and that the Father is seeking true worshippers who will do it right. Truth is prerequisite for true worship. To worship God, a person must understand Him in the truth of who He is and what He has done. A man's heart overflows with praise for God as the apprehension of truth touches down in a heart in tune with the Spirit of God. This is exactly the mind of the apostle in Ephesians 1 as he is enumerating the spiritual blessings that have been bestowed on him and the Ephesian Christians from the Father of eternity. The blessing that tops the whole list of blessings and that captivates the entire "praise session" of the apostle is the blessing of election and predestination (Ephesians 1:4, 5). See what praise and worship the apostle enjoys as he bows before the sovereign God! Before the world was ever established, the Creator chose a people from among others and appointed them to become His children through salvation, which thing he did not because of our will, but because of the good pleasure of His will.

# UNCONDITIONAL ELECTION

The Father of our Lord Jesus Christ could have passed by every single person, thus leaving them to their just desert–condemnation and wrath. But He acted with free and distinguishing grace to save some of the wicked and raise up a godly seed for the glory of His grace. The apostle worships the Sovereign with unbounded praise out of a heart of humility and gratitude, that though sinful and hell-deserving as others, God had mercy to make him accepted in the Beloved (Ephesians 1:6). Does the reader see how the doctrine of Election induced a greater swell of praise and worship in the apostle? Have you ever worshipped as the apostle in praising God especially for your election and predestination?

We see Moses communing with the God of Sinai in Exodus 33. After witnessing the awesome displays of His glorious power and unapproachable holiness, Moses, from a posture of entrancing admiration and worship, pleaded with God to show him a direct appearance of His essential glory. Jehovah responds affirmatively by saying in verse 19, "I will make all my goodness to pass before you, and I will proclaim the name of the Lord to you. I will be gracious to whom I will be gracious, and I will have compassion on whom I will have compassion." Dear friend, do you see that God's glory is a sovereign glory? The epitome of God's glory is best realized in God's sovereign and distinguishing grace to those sinners He determines to save. God is saying that His goodness and His name are the summary expressions of His sovereign display of electing love. If the reader will worship and praise the Lord for His goodness and lift high His exalted name, he should understand that this is done in recognition of the grace and compassion that flow out of His electing purpose.

These very words are later quoted by the apostle Paul in

Romans 9:15 as he defends God's sovereign election. Men, by nature, see election as partiality that diminishes God's love to unfairness or arbitrariness, which could never be praised. But Moses and Paul found exactly the opposite. Their worship was enhanced. Their hearts boiled over all the more. In their eyes, God was more exalted, glorious, and set apart than ever.

Dear reader, after having read Exodus 33:19 and Ephesians 1:4-6, do you honestly believe that you can understand the glory of God without understanding something of the sovereign, electing purpose of God in saving sinners? God has stated in no uncertain terms, "I will have mercy on whom I will have mercy, and I will have compassion on whom I will have compassion." Is there any Christian who should not be able to rejoice in this truth and bless the Lord in heartfelt worship, without the slightest doubtful stuttering?

Do we dare decide that this aspect of God's revealed nature is "not essential"—"unimportant"—"too divisive"—"good for nothing"—as some have decided, and therefore unworthy of our humble worship? The Word of God is not a smorgasbord counter where we choose only the more chewable, palatable, and tasty items of truth. C. H. Spurgeon spoke of what he believed was the reason for the church's ineffectiveness:

> "There has sprung up in the Church of Christ an idea that there are many things taught in the Bible which are not essential; that we may alter them just a little to suit our convenience: that provided we are right in the fundamentals, the other things are of no concern. . .But this know, that the slightest violation of the divine law will bring judgments upon the Church, and has brought judgments, and is even at this day witholding God's hand from blessing us. . .The Bible, the whole Bible,

and nothing but the Bible is the religion of Christ's Church. And until we come back to that the Church will have to suffer. . .

"Ah, how many have there been who have said, *'The old puritanic principles are too rough for these times; we'll alter them, we'll tone them down a little.'"* [75]

To either deny sovereign election or to store it away in some theological closet on shelves labeled "good for nothing," or "harmful," is to rob the people of God of the fullest view of God's glory and to limit the church's worship to the realms of human logic. Our worship, if *true* and *acceptable,* must be a response to and couched within the *whole truth* of who God is and what He has done.

The doctrine of election, properly understood, does exclude boasting and promote humility just as stated in the Southern Baptist statement of 1963. How essential to true worship are these conditions of heart! With such a glorious display of God's sovereign goodness, the human heart is bowed low before the Holy One, holding no claims, no rights, no pride whatsoever. The apostle taught in I Corinthians 1:24-31 that God has chosen and called us, and that if a man is in Christ it is not his own doing, but that of God's efficiency (v. 30). Every believer's boast and glory is not in himself, his flesh, his will, his parentage nor his choice (John 1:13; Romans 9:16), but in God alone. Let all glory be ascribed to the God who chose, predestined, and called out a worshipping people to bring praise to the glory of His grace. May the reader be brought to a more full expression of worship by embracing the *whole truth* of God's electing and redeeming grace. May all of us receive more enlightenment through wisdom and revelation by the Holy Spirit (Ephesians 1:17-23) to see

110

the big picture of God's redemptive plan and find our hearts bursting with praise for the Lord's sovereign salvation.

## UNDERSTANDING THE WHOLE BIBLE

One man said, "When I came to understand and embrace the doctrine of election, I got a whole new Bible." It is true. The Bible from Genesis to Revelation begins to open up with a new continuity and flow that a person cannot understand until he places election in right perspective. Looking at the Scriptures without that solid, unbroken vein of God's sovereign purpose running right down the center of redemptive history leaves one with a fragmented revelation from a less-than-sovereign deity. Our God is not bounced around by the will of man, nor foiled in His purpose by circumstances out of His control, nor does He ever have to resort to plan B because plan A failed. Our God has run His creation smoothly according to His purpose, and not one tick of the timepiece of His eternal purpose has ever been lost (Ephesians 1:11). Placing the hub of the covenant of grace at the center of the wheel brings unity, balance, and flow to an otherwise halting and unpredictable revelation. The whole Bible fits.

C. H. Spurgeon spoke of this foundational truth of election dispelling confusion and opening the Bible up with a view of the whole redemptive plan:

> "Without it there is a lack of unity of thought, and generally speaking they have no idea whatever of a system of divinity. It is almost   impossible to make a man a theologian unless you begin with this. You may if you please put a young believer to college for years,

but unless you show him this ground-plan of the ever-lasting covenant, he will make little progress, because his studies do not cohere, he does not see how one truth fits with another, and how all truths must harmonize together. Once let him get a clear idea that salvation is by grace, let him discover the difference between the covenant of works and the covenant of grace; let him clearly understand the meaning of election, as showing the purpose of God, and its bearing upon other doctrines which shew the accomplishment of that purpose, and from that moment he is on the high road to become an instructive believer. He will always be ready to give a reason of the hope that is in him with meekness and with fear. The proof is palpable. Take any county through-out England, you will find poor men hedging and ditching that have a better knowledge of divinity than one half of those who come from our academies and colleges, for the reason simply and entirely that these men have first learned in their youth the system of which election is a centre, and have afterwards found their own experience exactly square with it. They have built upon that good foundation a temple of holy knowledge, which has made them fathers in the Church of God. Every other scheme is as nothing to build with, they are but wood, hay, and stubble. Pile what you will upon them, and they will fall. They have no system of architecture; they belong to no order of reason or revelation. A disjointed system makes its topstone bigger than its foundation; it makes one part of the covenant to disagree with another; it makes Christ's mystical body to be of no shape whatever; it gives Christ a bride whom he does not know and does not choose, and it puts him up in the world to be married to any one who will have him; but he is to have no choice himself. It spoils every figure that is used with reference to Christ and his Church. The good old plan of the doctrines of grace is a system which when once received is seldom given up; when rightly learned, it moulds the thoughts of the heart, and it gives a sacred stamp to the characters of those who have once discovered its power."[76]

Many avoid the doctrine of election and predestination for fear of its depth–its technicality–supposing that they will "keep it simple," and avoid "hard theology". Modern pulpits hope to make the Bible easier to understand. The opposite effect takes place. Many parts of the Bible are impossible to understand, not to mention trying to explain, because the scope and sequence of revealed truth has been chopped up into a disorderly maze. Christians are left to a milk that fails to line up with much of Bible truth. When a person can embrace Unconditional Election, others become amazed at the level of understanding that person displays. He grows at an unprecedented rate of speed. He reads the books of history–they are his. He reads the prophets–they are his. He reads the books of poetry–they are his. The New Testament fits with the Old. Jesus' teachings–the parables, the kingdom, His eternal purpose, His work at Calvary –they all fit and they are his. This man may be a common laborer who knows nothing of "Bible College," and yet he excels in his knowledge of truth. The key to such a handle on the Bible as a whole is understanding God's divine and eternal theme which runs incessantly from Genesis through Revelation.

# UNCONDITIONAL ELECTION

## EVANGELISM

One of the first objections to the doctrine of election made by its enemies is the supposed effect it would have on evangelism. It is assumed by those trained in Arminian or pseudo-Calvinistic positions that to believe sovereign election, we would render evangelism unnecessary–or, at least, impotent. To many who name Christ's name, election *must be* incompatible with a heartfelt passion for hell-bound souls. How could we possibly give a sincere and free offer of the Gospel to every creature on God's earth? To embrace Unconditional Election *would have* to mean throwing the Great Commission in the refrigerator of hyper-Calvinism for cold storage and exclusivism. We can already hear the churches responding with "If they're going to be saved anyway, why be bothered with the urgency or task of world missions? It is hard enough trying to get the church burdened and mobilized for outreach as it is. This doctrine would once and for all kill, bury, and be done with the greatest commission Christ gave to His church–to reach a lost world with the gospel."

I would like to offer the reasons of God's word and from history as to why evangelism's greatest supporter, defender, interpreter, and motivator is none other than the doctrine of Unconditional Election. Brother Gambrell certainly agreed. Furthermore, I am convinced that great damage can come to many undiscerning souls by not being taught the fullness of gospel truth. This is not to say that many have not become Christians through preaching which is unfamiliar with or even opposed to Unconditional Election. But it is to say that with the various factors involved, gospel preaching not founded upon God's sovereign work of grace in the soul has caused much damage in Christ's church. It has populated the church with an over-abundance of unregenerate professors of salvation who show no life-changing fear toward or love for God.

## Our Lord's Command

Our sovereign Lord of the harvest has not only established His eternal purpose to save certain and specific sinners by His grace, but, also, He has ordained the means by which they will be converted to Him. He has commissioned His church in no uncertain terms to proclaim the "good news" of the gospel. The church has been given the task and privilege to command all men everywhere to repent and to trust Christ alone for salvation. We see these commands throughout the Scriptures, and these commands alone ought to be sufficient reason to evangelize even if we humanly cannot reconcile this duty with God's sovereign election. Such passages include Matthew 28:18-20; Mark 16:15; Luke 24:46, 47; Acts 1:8; I Corinthians 9:19-27; II Corinthians 5:18-20; and II Timothy 4:5.

We can also be assured that no one will be converted to Christ without the gospel being presented to him in some way (Romans 10:13-15). Missions is absolutely imperative in God's sovereign plan to save *His people* from their sin. He has so designed redemption that no one may be saved without believing the gospel of Christ, including the heathen who have never heard.

## Guaranteed Success

We freely send the gospel call to *every person* in the earth. We do not try to determine their elect/non-elect status before offering the gospel. There are no national boundaries, a more likely color of skin, or any discrimination whatsoever toward individuals to whom we make known the gospel. God "will gather His elect from the four winds, from one end of heaven to the other" (Matthew 24:31). His redeemed elect will represent every tribe, tongue, people, and nation of the earth in a heaven of glory (Revelation 5:9)–and He will use His church to bring the strangers home.

Jesus said in John 6:37, "All that the Father gives me *shall* come to me." We sow the seed of the Gospel with the certainty that all Christ's sheep *will* hear His voice and they *will* follow Him (John 10:27). Success in evangelism is not dependent on my persuasion, my skill, my programming, my personality. Success in evangelism is in God's hands. He alone can open a Lydia's heart. He alone can transform a Saul of Tarsus. He alone can bring repentance to a captive (II Timothy 2:25). We plant and water. It is God alone who gives the increase (I Corinthians 1:30). It is solely *of Him* that we are in Christ Jesus (I Corinthians 1:30)–and nothing of ourselves. He makes His people willing in the day of His power (Psalm 110:3), and *causes* the man whom He has chosen to come to Him (Psalm 65:4). Whether men reject or receive the gospel, the faithful gospel-sower is a victor (II Corinthians 2:14-17). Our first and last duty is to be faithful in the sight of God as a diffuser of the fragrance of Christ to all around us. In this we triumph, not in the securing of results (decisions) ourselves.

What a great encouragement! We know that God will save His people. We know that as we proclaim the great invitations of the Bible–Isaiah 55:1-3, "Ho, everyone who is thirsty, come to the waters . . ."; Matthew 11:28, "Come unto me, all you who are weary and heavy laden . . ."; and Revelation 22:17, "The

Spirit and the bride say, 'Come!' And let him who hears say, 'Come!' And let him who thirsts come. And whoever desires, let him take the water of life freely."–we are assured that God's elect will eventually respond (Acts 13:48).

Every soul who has been foreloved and predestinated *will, without exception, respond* to the powerful call of the Holy Spirit as the gospel is preached (Romans 8:29, 30). If folks do not respond to the gospel, the fault is not in a weak, helpless gospel or in an impotent savior who can do nothing to budge sovereign man (Romans 9:6-16). Man's response to the gospel is bound up in a sovereign God, and His purpose of election (Romans 9:11-24), which is true not only for the Jews, but also for the gentiles of all nations.

**Keep the Standard High**

God saves men by His truth. Our duty is to deliver the truth, the whole truth, and nothing but the truth. Please do not read into this statement a lack of love. In matters of such eternal importance it is less than true love that would not be completely honest with people about their souls. We are not peddling the Word of God (II Corinthians 2:17), nor do we hide or disguise any part of the gospel–that would be dishonest (II Corinthians 4:2, 3). Paul said, "We speak the truth in love" (Ephesians 4:15), but we must make certain that we speak the whole truth.

Jesus set the tone by preaching repentance and also by pressing repentance. He didn't leave the doctrine of repentance in the pulpit. He applied the implications of repentance to individual hearers. He pressed the rich young ruler about his god of material wealth. He pressed the woman at the well concerning her life of lust. He warned any who would be His followers that it would mean self-denial, dying to self, and devoted obedience if they would be true Christians (Luke 9:23-26). He called folks to count the costs of a disciple's life of hardships (Luke 9:57, 58; 14:25-33) in such a way that it appears at times that He tried to talk men *out* of following Him. Jesus was painfully honest about specific matters of sin and obedience. The Master Fisherman used the Ten Commandments in evangelism to let people see how their lives were an offense to a holy God, how disobedient they were, how guilty they were and what a life of righteousness really consisted of.

Today, because of our silence about repentance, the gospel has been cheapened. Our membership rolls are filled with many people we cannot find, and many others who show no evangelical obedience to Christ. According to Sunday School Board statistics, 49.3% of the baptized membership of the Southern Baptist Convention in 1985 did not participate in <u>any activity</u> at the churches of which they were members. The Church Training Department has even begun a program to reclaim inactive church members. This figure does not account for members who attend a service occasionally and others who have no involvement in Christ's Kingdom. The average SBC church has only 20-30 per cent of its "members" actively serving Christ, and yet many boast of their great memberships. How did the churches get so top-heavy with uncaring, unspiritual, disobedient professors?

The pulpits have gone "soft" in laying out the demands of the gospel by shelving the all-important truth of repentance. The modern gospel of "accept Jesus" is simply a watered down result of unwillingness to preach the necessity of repentance. Modern pulpits, attempting to stimulate sinners into a "decision for Christ" are generally afraid to lay out the costs of discipleship

# ELECTION AND EVANGELISM

because of the probability of turning away many that otherwise would boost baptism ratios and attendance campaigns.

It is presumed that to press repentance we would establish a "works salvation." Yet we cannot reconcile the methods Jesus used in His own evangelism to accepted methods today. By our evangelical standards today, Jesus really should have won the rich young ruler. The young man wanted to go to heaven. He even appealed directly to Jesus for the way to eternal life. Any honest preacher today knows that in most churches the young man of Mark 10:17 would have been ushered into a counseling room, given four things to know, and led in a prayer of decision. He would be encouraged to be regular in Sunday School and Church Training in order to find out what had happened to him and how to grow in his new-found faith. After all, he could deal with his greed and love of money later as he grew.

How different this scheme of evangelism is from that of our Lord. The Lord Jesus, in Luke 9:23, 24, said that a man cannot be considered a Christian until there is a radical resignation of self and a surrender of life to the daily authority of God's Word. There must be a radical change in a person's thinking that will radically change his lifestyle.

The evangelism of Jesus shows the superficiality of today's shallow, soul-deceiving appeals, such as "simply believe" and "all you have to do is ask Jesus into your heart." What would happen to our baptism statistics if we laid out the gospel demands as Jesus did? The number of people not interested in being seriously obedient to Christ as Lord after their supposed conversion is staggering. The churches are blamed for poor follow-up programs—for "winning them and dropping them," as if a super follow-up program will produce heart convictions in a dead soul that now is under the pretence of a genuine conver-

119

sion. God's Word does not teach, offer, or insinuate "follow-up" programs. If people were truly born of the Spirit, there was no need for appeals or programs to entice their attendance and devotion. Lowering the standard of gospel evangelism with man's shallow techniques and candy-coated appeals may boost per-capita baptism ratios but will fill the pews of hell with the self-deceived. By introducing the gospel with the word "repent," Jesus did His "follow-up" work <u>prior</u> to conversion.

Unconditional Election encourages us to keep the standard of evangelism as high as that of Christ. We should have no fear of turning men away with an unnecessarily "hard requirement" if it is compatible with Christ's own practice. Repentance, being a response to God's sovereign work of regeneration in the soul, will come if God is pleased to save a person. God uses the gospel of repentance to change the heart inside.

**Aim For the Heart**

Unconditional Election directs us to go for the heart of a man in the preaching of the gospel. The will of man is not to be the center of attention. "Decisions" for Christ are not our main target. As we have seen, man's heart problem is much more incapacitating than would afford him the ability to just decide to exercise his unfree will. J. I. Packer speaks to the error of aiming at man's will:

"Let us work this out. If we regarded it as our job, not simply to present Christ, but actually to produce converts–to evangelize, not only faithfully, but also successfully–our approach to evangelism would become pragmatic and calculating. We should conclude that our basic equipment, both for personal dealing and for public preaching, must be twofold. We must have, not merely a clear grasp of the meaning and application of the gospel, but also an irresistible technique for inducing a response. We should, therefore, make it our business to try and develop such a technique. And we should evaluate all evangelism, our own and other people's by the criterion, not only of the message preached, but also of visible results. If our own efforts were not bearing fruit, we should conclude that our technique still needed improving. If they were bearing fruit, we should conclude that this justified the technique we had been using. We should regard evangelism as an activity involving a battle of wills between ourselves and those to whom we go, a battle in which victory depends on our firing off a heavy enough barrage of calculated effects. Thus our philosophy of evangelism would become terrifyingly similar to the philosophy of brainwashing. And we would no longer be able to argue, when such a similarity is asserted to be a fact, that this is not a proper conception of evangelism. For it *would be* a proper conception of evangelism, if the production of converts was really our responsibility.

This shows us the danger of forgetting the practical implications of God's sovereignty. It is right to recognize our responsibility to engage in aggressive evangelism. It is right to desire the conversion of unbelievers. It is right to want one's presentation of the gospel to be as clear and forcible as possible. If we preferred that converts should be few and far between, and did not care whether our proclaiming of Christ went home or not, there would be something wrong with us. But it is not right when we take it on us to do more than God has given us to do. It is not right when we regard ourselves as responsible for securing converts, and look to our own enterprise and techniques to accomplish what only God can accomplish. To do that is to intrude ourselves into the office of the Holy Ghost, and to exalt ourselves as the agents of the new birth.

And the point that we must see is this: *only by letting our knowledge of God's sovereignty control the way in which we plan, and pray, and work in His service, can we avoid becoming guilty of this fault.* For where we are not consciously relying on God, there we shall inevitably be found relying on ourselves. And the spirit of self-reliance is a blight on evangelism. Such, however, is the inevitable consequence of forgetting God's sovereignty in the conversion of souls." [77]

Our main objective in heart evangelism is twofold: to bring the law of a sovereign and righteous God to bear upon a sinner's heart to the point of desperation, and to direct the sinner to flee to Christ in a total abandonment of sin and self to plead for mercy and for a new life. The key word that we are after in this objective is "desperation." Sinners must be brought by the Holy Spirit to be desperate. Inherent in the very nature of fleeing to Christ is desperation (Hebrews 6:18). Look at every conversion in the Scripture and you see desperation after God's mercy in the man's soul. Whether folks were bitten by serpents or listening to Peter at Pentecost, be it a Philippian jailer or a blind Bartimaeus, there was desperation after mercy. Dr. Martyn Lloyd-Jones said, "It is made perfectly clear in the pages of the New Testament that no man can be saved until, at some time or other, he has felt desperate about himself." [78] If partially-fallen man has a sovereign will to decide for Christ anytime he pleases, there is no desperation.

The divine method we are to employ in evangelism is a *God-centered* approach and not a man-centered one. Our choice of approach, based upon theology, will determine what we want the sinner to know and feel. If the sinner is made to *know* and *feel* what he needs to know and feel by the regenerating work of the Spirit, he will make a right decision. No one will have to talk him into doing anything. He will certainly not grip the pew with unbelieving reluctance until his knuckles turn white before he finally gives in. The Scripture knows nothing of such conversions.

Desperation is the key. How do we evangelize in order to see a sinner brought to desperation? We lay out Bible truths with compassionate concern in full dependence upon God's Spirit to sovereignly take them to the heart. These Bible truths include the following:

1. The Nature of God – People need to understand something of who God is as Creator, Sovereign Sustainer, Lawgiver, Judge, and Savior. This is exactly where Paul began every time he presented the gospel to untaught gentiles (Acts 17:22-31). Men need to be bowed before God's righteous majesty and see Him as Moses described–"Glorious in holiness, fearful in praises, doing wonders."

2. The Holy Law of God – People should understand something of their transgressions and offenses before this Holy God as revealed through the Law (Romans 3:19, 20). They need to understand how the law has been broken, not only by outward actions, but by the heart in desires and motives (Matthew 5:22, 28). They need to see not only their guilt as lawbreakers, but also

their inward corruption, bondage, and vile nature. The law must do the work in them as it did in Paul (Romans 7:7-13) until they see their sin as *exceeding sinful*. Fearful desperation needs to bring trembling men before a Holy Sovereign who is angry with them as they take each breath. Is this not the very language of the sweet singer of Israel in Psalm 5:4-6 and 7:ll, l2? Did not John the Baptist warn of the wrath of God presently on the head of every sinner (John 3:36)? And was it not the Apostle Paul in New Testament fashion who said that sinners are presently treasuring up for themselves wrath against the day of wrath (Romans 2:5)? Every man's sin is great in the eyes of the Lawgiver.

**3.** <u>Jesus Christ–Crucified and Risen</u> – The only remedy for a lost man is found in Jesus. His atoning blood is the only refuge for a guilty man. His shed blood is the only cleansing agent to purge and wash a soul clean. His righteousness freely given to sinners is the only way to be made accepted with God. Only through the risen Christ is there victory over sin and the grave. He alone gives new life and new freedom. Only Jesus! Only Jesus! Only Jesus! (John l4:6)

**4.** <u>Man's Duty–Repent and Believe</u> – The only person to be saved is the person who radically turns from sin and trusts in Christ. This is a duty and is given as a command. God's Word promises the sinner salvation only on these gospel terms and not upon anything less than these terms. God, in His love, will receive sinners with open arms and will cast none away, but only those will be received who come on His terms. Salvation's benefits should not be dangled before the sinner as an appealing bait with which to hook him. He must repent and believe even if there were far less benefits than there are. Emphasizing benefits only capitalizes on a sinner's selfish condition.

5.  Sovereign Mercy – The "boxing up" principle [79] is leaving men in the hands of God at this point, having explained the gospel and having urged them to repent and believe. We err by explaining precise movements and by giving explicit directions to a sinner as to how to come to Christ, as though he will bring about his own regeneration. Often people walk an aisle or pray a prayer to come to Christ, assuming *they did* what was required, and we have effectively turned salvation by grace into salvation by works. They think that because *they took* the instructed steps that they have obtained a change of heart. The counselors are careful to tell them that they "must mean it with all their hearts," but the question remains, "How do we or *they* know if they mean a sinner's prayer with all their hearts?" Didn't Jeremiah say, "The heart is deceitful above all things and desperately wicked; who can know it?" How do we know this person is not a stony-ground hearer or a thorny-ground hearer as he received the gospel (Matthew 13:3-23)? So often, in our sincere desire to see men converted, we prematurely abort the necessary work to be done in the heart by explicit instructions that we hope will bring a true heart conversion. The sinner just needs to be left in the hands of the sovereign God and if God is pleased to save him, we will know it by the desperation after Himself that will be evident.

The "boxing up" principle is putting the sinner into

the pressure cooker of divine grace with several other ingredients. These include God's Law, God's Love and Grace, and God's Sovereignty.

**A.** *God's Law* – After the gospel presentation, we must pray that God will bring about the powerful, yet painful, agonizing effect that Paul described (Romans 7:7-13). There must be contrition and sorrow for sin, not because sin has hurt us, but because our sin has displeased God. This will provide the basis for true heart repentance. The old divines termed this heart activity as "law work," and it must operate deeply and thoroughly.

**B.** *God's Love and Grace* – There is mercy with the Lord. There is salvation through Christ. The sinner must be made to believe the person and work of Christ is God's demonstration of wondrous love and the only provision for man's sin and salvation. "But God demonstrates His own love toward us, in that while we were still sinners, Christ died for us (Romans 5:8)." The infinite and loving grace of God was manifested as a certainty chiefly when God sent His own Son to be the propitiation for our sins (I John 4:10). No greater love has ever existed!

**C.** *God's Sovereignty* – Man must also understand that he is locked up on death row without a key. God has the key. Man does not decide anything. He should be told of all the things he cannot do.

1. He cannot understand - I Corinthians 2:14
2. He cannot hear - John 8:43
3. He cannot see - John 3:3
4. He cannot come - John 6:44

5. He cannot be subject to God's Law - Romans 8:7

He should be told "God will have mercy on whom He will have mercy and He will have compassion on whom He will have compassion" (Romans 9:15). He should be reduced to utter hopelessness and helplessness apart from the sovereign mercy and grace of God. The decision is in God's hands–to harden the sinner's heart by leaving him to his natural desires and free choices to perish in hell, or to grant to him the free grace of repentance and saving faith as a gift that will glorify His own name in the ages to come (Ephesians 2:7-9).

You see, in this presentation there are no bargaining tables, no truces, or peace treaties. The sinner falls humbly before the throne of an exalted Christ to beg for mercy. Salvation is in the hands of a sovereign Christ (John 17:2), and He will give it to whomever He is pleased to give it (John 5:21).

This *does not* mean the Lord is reluctant to receive sinners. He stands ready graciously to receive all who flee to Him in the desperation of repentance and faith. The fact remains, no man will flee to Christ except the Spirit bring him. This work of the Spirit is at the sovereign disposal of the Almighty.

## "God's Just Liberty"

Jonathan Edwards preached sermons to the cold and dead churches of New England. The Almighty was pleased to use these sermons in the converting of many and the spread of a "Great Awakening." While Edwards preached the truth of justification by faith alone (which was rare in these churches) he was convincing men of the futility of works to earn God's favor or to obligate God's blessing. Many present-day evangelists would say "yea and amen!" However, Edwards followed up these discourses with others in which he taught God's *"absolute sovereignty in regard to the salvation of sinners and His just liberty in regard to answering the prayers of mere natural man.*

The idea of "God's just liberty" was a powerful part of Edwards' gospel presentation. It included all that is meant in the doctrine of election. This is what Edwards meant by "God's just liberty"–First, God's liberty is *perfect*. There is nothing the natural man has done or can do to impair or bind God to decide favorably in his case. God is at perfect liberty to grant the sinner "saving faith" and "heart repentance" or to withold such grace. The sinner may repeat the "sinner's prayer" over and over *to no avail* if God does not grant a changed heart by the new birth. The sinner may call on the name of the Lord and never receive the saving mercy that leads to real conversion (Matthew 7:21).

Secondly, God's liberty is also *just*. Joseph Tracy analyzed Edwards' use of "God's just liberty" in this way:

"Sinners have merited and now deserve instant damnation; and God's liberty to inflict it upon them now, or defer it for the present, or save them from it wholly, according to his own pleasure, is a most "just liberty." When the sinner sees and feels this doctrine to be true, he knows that no course remains for him, but to call upon God for mercy; and he knows that when he calls upon God, there is nothing in his prayers that at all impairs God's "just liberty" with respect to hearing him, and that he has nothing to depend upon, as a ground of hope that he shall be heard, but the mercy of God in Christ. He can make no appeal to the justice of God, for that only condemns him; nor to any other attribute but mercy, which, in its very nature, is free, and not constrained. And he can find no satisfactory evidence that God is disposed to be merciful to sinners, but in the fact that he has given his Son to die for them. Here is his only ground of hope. Here he must present and urge his prayer, knowing that he deserves to be rejected, and knowing that nothing of his own, not even his prayer, diminishes God's 'just liberty', to receive or reject him according to his good pleasure. And this is the point to which he needs to be brought. This is the dependence which he needs to feel, the very feeling which will drive him to God in prayer.

"It teaches him to resign himself to the disposal of God, sensible of God's 'just liberty,' and not knowing first what God will do with him; but encouraged by the goodness of God as shown in the death of his Son, to hope for acceptance and salvation. And this is faith; and faith 'works by love,' and transforms the whole character." [80]

It was when men like Edwards began preaching such sermons in the 1730's that the "Spirit of God began extraordinarily to set in and wonderfully to work among us" and many began to be savingly converted.

This is a far cry from the modern appeals to sovereign sinners to decide to open their heart's door and *let* the poor, helpless, handcuffed Jesus come in. Men are told, "God has done all He can do; now it is all up to you." This is nonsense! Was this the impotent Jesus that confronted Saul of Tarsus and summoned him to repent and obey from that day forward? Man is not on the throne–only the LORD!

As the Holy Spirit uses the powerful truth of "God's just

liberty" the sinner is made to fear for his soul. His hands are emptied of all possible plans or schemes to deal with the matter of his soul at a more convenient time. He is made to see the mercy of God as the only hope for his guilty, sin-laden soul, and that it is very possible that the sovereign God will give him what he justly deserves in spite of formal petitions for salvation. He is made to see that *even his prayers and petitions to God for salvation can be of a self-serving nature* rather than of true heart repentance and faith which alone result in a changed life. He is made to see that God is not obligated to give salvation even though he takes all the "required" steps.

He is reduced to the position of a <u>Bartimaeus</u> who had no idea whether the Messiah would stop and have mercy upon him. Bartimaeus was desperate enough that he began to cry out, and continued to cry out until the Savior stopped. How presumptuous sinners are today who think, "Of course Jesus will save me –I asked Him to, didn't I?" This is not the faith of Bartimaeus.

If God is pleased to save a man, these truths will be taken to the heart with the result of desperation. The pressure cooker of Divine Grace will have done its work. This is not saying that all sinners are saved by the same outward experience, by the same Scripture verses, or in the same time sequence. God's mysterious work is as varied as every fingerprint. In fact, it is much of modern evangelism that simply gives the same presentation of the same three or four points to every individual in a canned approach. Our Lord's evangelism began with a varied approach every time, depending on the individual's starting point. Nevertheless, everyone who is truly converted was eventually brought to the same place–desperation. We want to see sinners get to the place where the leper was–". . . Lord, if thou wilt, thou canst make me clean" (Luke 5:12); and where Barti-maeus was—"Jesus, thou son of David, have mercy on me" (Mark 10:47); and where the publican was—". . . God be merciful to me a sinner" (Luke 18:13). This is how God uses the "boxing up" principle. We can only shut sinners up to God and His truth, stand back and see the salvation of the Lord!

## Altar Call

These are the very reasons why I do not employ an "altar call" after preaching the gospel. First, there was *never* any directive or example given in Scripture for the use of altar calls. In fact, the Christian Church knew nothing of an altar call for over 1800 years. Surprisingly enough, people were converted without them for many years, and the church did just fine. This, of course, is an understatement. The Gospel under the Spirit's power was sufficient to transform lives through the ages without the church having to adopt extra-Biblical measures.

In addition, this "mechanistic" approach easily falls into a "works salvation" trap. Much like those who pretend to be regenerated through baptism, there are many who attribute their new birth to walking the aisle, agreeing with the counselor's presentation, and praying a prayer. As Spurgeon and others fought the heresy of "baptismal regeneration," so we would not want to be guilty of a "decisional regeneration." God, not man's will, blows the new birth upon the soul by His sovereign grace (John 3:8). Anyone can take these mechanical steps and yet how duped they are to think that because they took the required steps, they will receive the new birth. These directions have the effect, not of throwing men upon God for His mercy, but of throwing themselves upon their own acts.

In the third place, sinners should be left "boxed up" with

# UNCONDITIONAL ELECTION

God's Law, God's Love and Grace, and God's Sovereignty until God has brought new life to the heart. We short-circuit what good has been done in the preaching by *setting up* an immediate response. We are duty-bound to call for an immediate response of repentance and faith, but we have no authority to do the Holy Spirit's work in setting up and walking a sinner through what we think will effect heart regeneration.

Fourthly, the public profession of faith is done at baptism. This is exactly the purpose that baptism was given to accomplish. Baptism is God's appointed means to publicly confess the Lord, not an altar call.

Fifthly, the gospel is no less proclaimed without an altar call. The good news is to be heartily and boldly set forth. The warnings and promises, the duties and blessings of the Gospel, and all the appropriate applications of the gospel are to be declared with a burning passion and a holy urgency. We are to pray for burdened hearts, crying to God for the lost to be saved, much like John Knox did when he said, "Give me Scotland or I die!"

The following thoughts on presenting the gospel to sinners are from Dr. Asahel Nettleton. This nineteenth-century evangelist from the New England area stood in contrast to his more popular contemporary, Charles Finney. Though Nettleton was believed to be the means of bringing no less than thirty-thousand souls to Christ, his memory and methods are conveniently laid to rest in a Christian culture known for its shortcuts and doctrinal superficiality. Nettleton's obscurity, next to Finney, was largely due to his Calvinistic and careful style of evangelism. In contrast to Finney, Nettleton would have nothing to do with the "new measures" of bringing men to Christ, namely the employment of altar calls. He believed the "new measures" to be "calamitous" and opposed to careful, heart-searching evangelism. Let us hear his comments and those about him made by other men on the gospel concepts raised in this book. May I urge the reader to compare them with those of J. B. Gambrell. These quotes are taken from <u>The Life and Labors of Asahel Nettleton:</u>

"He (Nettleton) felt it to be of the first importance to preach the doctrines of grace with great plainness in revivals of religion. He had no confidence in those revivals in which these doctrines could not be preached. His opinion was, that while the preaching of divine sovereignty and election, with their kindred doctrines, was eminently fitted to check fanaticism, and put a period to a spurious religious excitement, it was equally adapted to promote a genuine revival of religion."

Nettleton explained:

"I have seen churches run down by repeated excitements, in which there was *emotion* merely, without *instruction*." "In the first stage of a revival," said he, "while depravity is yet ascendant, and conscience asleep, I would preach the Law, with its awful sanctions and solemn claims on sinners to be holy, and that immediately. But when the first moments of a revival are past, and sinners are settling down on presumptuous confidences, I would preach Election. Conscience is then roused enough to make a cord which sinners cannot break. Their own convictions are on my side, so that they cannot escape; and I would hold them fast, and repeat my strokes under the fire and hammer of divine truth."

"He (Nettleton) was cautious in admitting persons to the Church. He would not encourage any to make a profession of religion till they gave satisfactory evidence of a change of heart."

"In his (Nettleton's) own management in times of revivals, by preaching and personal intercourse, nothing was more deserving of being studied and imitated, than his *thoroughness, caution, and discrimination.* In these respects there was a heaven-wide difference between Dr. Nettleton and some of the most noted of his professed imitators. Being thoroughly 'rooted and grounded in the truth' himself, his presentations of it were clear, pungent, and searching. His revival topics were systematically and admirably arranged. In his discourses he began at the beginning. A full believer in the total depravity of the human heart, he arraigned sinners, whether young or old, as rebels against God; and made the threatenings of the law thunder in their ears, as but few preachers have power to do. With him, acting as an ambassador of Christ, there was no such thing as compromise. The rebels must 'throw down their arms,' and submit unconditionally, or he would give them no hope of pardon. Hundreds, if not thousands, can witness what a terrible dissector he was of the 'joints and the marrow.' At the same time that he shewed the impenitent they were lost, he made them feel that they had 'destroyed themselves.' It was difficult to say which he made plainest—their danger or their guilt; their immediate duty to repent, or the certainty that, without being drawn and renewed by the Spirit of God, *they never would repent.* It was in vain for them to retreat from one refuge to another. He was sure to strip them of all their vain excuses, and deliver them over to their consciences, to be dealt with according to law and justice. He preached what are called the hard doctrines—such as divine sovereignty, election, and regeneration—with great plainness, discrimination, and power. His grand aim was to instruct, convince, and persuade; to this end his appeals were constantly made to the understanding, the conscience, and the heart. The passions he never addressed, nor were his discourses at all calculated to excite them. Any outbreak of mere animal feeling he was always afraid of, as tending to warp the judgment and beget false hopes. His grand aim was to instruct his hearers as thoroughly, and point out the difference between true and spurious conversion so clearly, as to make it difficult for them to get hopes at all without good spiritual evidence on which to found them. Knowing how apt persons are to cling to their hopes, whether good or bad, he depended much more upon holding them back, till they had good evidence, than upon shaking them from their false foundations."

"The chief excellence of his preaching seemed to consist in great plainness and simplicity, and discrimination—in much solemnity and affectionate earnestness of manner—in the application of the truth to the heart and conscience—in taking away the excuses of sinners, and leaving them without help and hope, except in the sovereign mercy of God. In short, it was conformed to the work for which the Spirit was sent into the world,—viz., to reprove or convince the world of Sin, of Righteousness, and of Judgment. This characteristic was most striking. His manner of dealing with awakened sinners was peculiar. While it served to deepen their convictions, and lead them to Christ, it gained their confidence, and secured their belief of the truth. He knew, too, how to search those who expressed hope. And while he detected the hypocrite, and encouraged the desponding, he was regarded by all with affection and reverence."

"He (Nettleton) shewed the sinner that his unregenerate prayers for a new heart, his impenitent seeking, striving, and knocking, would be of no avail; and that absolute, unconditional submission to a sovereign God, was the first thing to be done . . ."

"His (Nettleton's) visits among the people were *frequent,* but *short and profitable.* He entered immediately on the subject of the salvation of the soul, and the great importance of attending to it without delay. He did not customarily propound questions and require answers, lest by this means he should turn the attention of sinners from their own wretched state, by leading them to think 'How they should reply to the minister.' He was so well acquainted with the human heart, that he seemed to have an intuitive perception of what was passing in the minds of those whom he was addressing. Thus he could so direct his conversation as to produce silence and self-condemnation, and confine their thoughts to their own lost and ruined state, sometimes remarking: *'You have no time to spend in conversation before the salvation of the soul is secured.'* When any indulged a hope which was not satisfactory, he would say: 'You had better give it up, and seek your salvation in earnest.'"

"A young female, who had been for some time in a

state of religious anxiety, said to him: 'What do you think of *the doctrine of Election?* Some say it is true; and some say it is not true, and I do not know what to think of it.'–'And what do you wish to think of it?' said Dr. Nettleton. 'I wish,' said she, 'to think that it is not true.'–'Suppose, then,' said Dr. Nettleton, 'that it is not true. The doctrine of repentance is true. You must repent or perish. Now, if the doctrine of election is not true, what reason have you to believe you ever shall repent?' After a moment's reflection, she replied: 'If the doctrine of election is not true, I never shall repent.' Her eyes were then opened upon her true condition. Every refuge failed her. She saw that she was entirely dependent on the sovereign grace of God; and, there is reason to believe, she was soon brought out of darkness into God's marvelous light."

One of Dr. Nettleton's contemporaries, Rev. Cobb, wrote concerning Nettleton's ministry:

"As the revival became more interesting and powerful, he preached more doctrinally. He brought from his treasure the doctrines of total depravity, personal election, reprobation, the sovereignty of divine grace, and the universal government of God in working all things after the counsel of His own will. And these great doctrines did not *paralyze*, but greatly *promote* the good work. *Never had brother Nettleton such power over my congregation, as when he poured forth in torrents these awful truths.* And at no time were converts multiplied so rapidly, and convictions and distress so deep, as when these doctrines were pressed home to the conscience."

# UNCONDITIONAL ELECTION

Nettleton wrote the following statement in his diary during a period of awakening in Nassau, New York during the month of April, 1820:

"I have since thought that the effect of my leaving them as I did —*in the advanced stages of their conviction* —was evidently beneficial. It drove them from all human dependence.

The following is an extract from the letter of an English preacher. He wrote it after observing several revival meetings in America. Nettleton concurred with him 100 percent.

"Terrific sermons and other means are artfully contrived to stimulate the feelings of ignorant people. In compliance with the call given at the period of the highest excitement, they repair to the *anxious seat* by scores. As their fears are soon aroused, they are generally as soon calmed; and in a few days many profess to entertain hope. Many such converts soon lose all appearance of religion; but they become conceited, secure, and Gospel-proof; so that, while living in the open and habitual neglect of their duty, they talk very freely of the time when they experienced religion."[81]

We have come to a point today that to imagine a Gospel meeting or church service without an altar call would be bordering on heresy or liberalism. Altar calls have become evangelicals' sign of "real evangelism." The presentation of the Gospel is not complete to many if the "sawdust trail" is not the great climax of a well-planned meeting.

However, not one word of the Holy Scripture supports such an "essential tradition." This practice is only the consistent outworking of Arminian theology–secure decisions. Altar calls are the invention of the Arminian delusion–"you can do it"–"you

138

can come to Christ"–"All you have to do is pray this prayer." While the Scriptures teach that men *must* flee to Christ, it also, in no uncertain terms, teaches that man *cannot* come to Christ. To concoct a method whereby men are "walked through" the prescribed steps to effect the new birth is to try to produce an effect which only the Sovereign Spirit of God can do. Arminians think that if men just pray the prayer, it all happens. How deceived we are! This was not the faith of our founding fathers, and it ought not to be today.

We must, with passionate entreaties, press men to flee to Christ. They must earnestly be urged to believe, to call, to cast their souls upon Jesus immediately. But for the Lord's sake and for the sake of deluded professors, let us not do anything in our evangelism that might contribute to the cauterizing of consciences due to the fact that they have made "their decision" for Christ by taking the required steps.

Please hear the words of C. H. Spurgeon on the issue of altar calls:

> "Let me say, very softly and whisperingly, that there are little things among ourselves which must be carefully looked after, or we shall have a leaven of Ritualism and priesthood working in our measures of meal. In our revival services, it might be as well to vary our procedure. Sometimes shut up that enquiry-room. I have my fears about that institution if it be used in permanence, and as an inevitable part of the services. It may be a very wise thing to invite persons who are under concern of soul to come apart from the rest of the congregation, and have conversation with godly people; but if you should ever see a notion is fashioning itself that there is something to be got in the private room which is not to

be had at once in the assembly, or that God is more at that penitent form than elsewhere, aim a blow at that notion at once. We must not come back by a rapid march to the old ways of altars and confessionals, and have a Romish trumpery restored in a coarser form. If we make men think that conversation with ourselves or with helpers is essential to their faith in Christ, we are taking the direct line for priestcraft. In the Gospel, the sinner and the Saviour are to come together, with none between. Speak upon this point very clearly. 'You, sinner, sitting where you are, believing on the Lord Jesus Christ, shall have eternal life. Do not stop till you pass into an enquiry room. Do not think it essential to confer with me. Do not suppose that I have the keys of the Kingdom of Heaven, or that these godly men and women associated with me can tell you any other Gospel than this. He that believeth on the Son hath everlasting life.'"

"'Go home alone, (he would say,) 'trusting in Jesus'. (Spurgeon now quotes the sinner) 'I would like to go into the enquiry room.' 'I dare say you would, but we are not willing to pander to popular superstition. We fear that in those rooms men are warmed into fictitious confidence. Very few of the supposed converts of enquiry rooms turn out well. Go to your God at once, even where you are now. Cast yourself on Christ, now, at once, ere you stir an inch!'"

"God has not appointed salvation by enquiry rooms . . . For the most part, a wounded conscience, like a wounded stag, delights to be alone that it may bleed in secret." [82]

# ELECTION AND EVANGELISM

Finally, the wisdom of D. Martyn Lloyd-Jones is clear as he writes in his book <u>Preaching and Preachers</u>. The "Doctor" was giving eight reasons against "calling for decisions".

"Most would agree with my sixth point which is that this method tends to produce a superficial conviction of sin, if any at all. People often respond because they have the impression that by doing so they will receive certain benefits. I remember hearing of a man who was regarded as one of the 'star converts' of a campaign. He was interviewed and asked why he had gone forward in the campaign the previous year. His answer was that the evangelist had said, 'If you do not want to "miss the boat" you had better come forward.' He said that he did not want to 'miss the boat' so he had gone forward; and all the interviewer could get out of him was that he somehow felt that he was now 'on the boat'. He was not clear about what this meant, not what it was, and nothing had seemed to happen to him during the subsequent year. But there it was; it can be as superficial as that.

". . . That is the kind of thing that may happen even when an appeal is not made. But when an appeal is made it is greatly exaggerated and so you get spurious conversions. As I have reminded you even John Wesley, the great Arminian, did not make appeals to people to 'come forward'. What you find so often in his Journals is something like this: 'Preached at such and such a place. Many seemed to be deeply affected, but God alone knows how deeply.' Surely that is very significant and important. He had spiritual understanding and knew that many factors can affect us. What he was

# UNCONDITIONAL ELECTION

concerned about was not immediate visible results but the work of the Holy Spirit in regeneration. A knowledge of the human heart, of psychology, should teach us to avoid anything that increases the possibility of spurious results." [83]

## Does Election Really Kill Evangelism?

It is often claimed that the preaching of doctrine and certainly the doctrine of Unconditional Election, will sap the church of evangelistic zeal and drive. Churches reportedly have grown ice-cold under the influence of this high doctrine.

If their claims be true, one searching question must be asked–What happened in the Southern Baptist Convention for eighty years? It has been clearly shown that Unconditional Election was the foundation of all doctrinal views that ignited the convention to be the great evangelistic and missionary force that it was. How did it happen? How did these "hyper-Calvinists" ever get untracked and have any evangelistic concern if these claims be true?

History provides all the evidence necessary to prove the ludicrous nature of such claims. Consider all the major missionary movements, along with the Great Awakenings in America. Consider the great Protestant Reformation in Europe. It is easily demonstrated that believers in Unconditional Election have led the way in missionary zeal and effort.

Spurgeon loved to speak to this topic:

"The greatest missionaries that have ever lived have believed in God's choice of them; and instead of this doctrine leading to inaction, it has ever been an irresistible motive power, and it will be so again. It was the secret energy of the Reformation. It is because free

142

grace has been put into the background that we have seen so little done in many places. It is in God's hand the great force which can stir the church of God to its utmost depth. It may not work superficial revivals, but for deep work it is invaluable. Side by side with the blood of Christ it is the world's hope. How can men say that the doctrine of distinguishing grace makes men careless about souls? Did they never hear of the evangelical band which was called the Clapham sect? Was Whitefield a man who cared nothing for the salvation of the people? He who flew like a seraph throughout England and America unceasingly proclaiming the grace of God, was he selfish? Yet he was distinctively a free-grace preacher. Did Jonathan Edwards have no concern for the souls of others? Oh, how he wept, and cried, and warned them of the wrath to come! Time would fail me to tell of the lovers of men who have been lovers of this truth." [84]

As Brother Gambrell indicated, if you really want to be invigorated in your faith and renewed in your courage to the task of evangelism, reflect upon how God has used the preaching of the historic doctrines of grace (election, predestination, etc.) to bring many to Himself in salvation!

PRAYER

While the natural mind asks, "Why pray for conversions if God will save whom He will?", the scriptural mind confesses,

# UNCONDITIONAL ELECTION

"The only gospel effectiveness we will have comes through prayer." It is not for us to ask why God has ordained that we should pray, as if prayer is a kind of administrative red tape.

We are wholly dependent upon our sovereign God to open the hearts of our hearers as He did with Lydia (Acts 16:14), without which we are those who possess a pure impotence in gospel labors. God will make us pray before He blesses our labors so that we constantly will be mindful of the One who really deserves the glory for results. God not only chooses to save the foolish, weak, and base of this world, that no flesh should glory in His presence (I Corinthians 1:26-29), but He is also pleased to use foolish, weak, and base vessels like you and me to declare His testimony with fear and trembling in the demonstration of the Spirit and power, that converted souls should not be attributed to our wisdom, but to the power of God (I Corinthians 2:1-5). God's power to save sinners is tapped only through fervent intercession and is applied consistently and *compatibly* with His purpose of sovereign election. Saving the sinners of His choice is His work. He commissions us to participate in His work through prayer and preaching.

Everyone is a Calvinist when on his knees in prayer. This is why we pray. We believe God alone can bring a sinner to salvation, and without God's grace a sinner will never repent and believe. You ask for God to draw sinners, break sinners, convince sinners, change the hearts of sinners, because you believe He is able and that He must. Why does He do it with some and not others? The answer is election—"And as many as had been ordained to eternal life believed" (Acts 13:48). But the same Apostle Paul, who wrote the two most prolific chapters on God's sovereign purpose of election in Romans 9 and 11, exposed the burden of his broken heart to see his countrymen saved in chapter 10. His only recourse was to pray (Romans 10:1). His only opportunity to vent a passion for his fellow Jews was before the throne of grace. Were his prayers for his friends' salvation only wishful thinking? Absolutely not! The same God who comforted Paul with the assurance of success in view of the conquering purpose of election (chapters 9 and 11), also ignited within Paul's soul a consuming desire to reach as many men as God would allow him to reach. Therefore he *prays* (10:1) and he *preaches* (10:8-15). He also enlists all the people of God to pray for gospel success in his missionary labors (II Thessalonians 3:1), knowing that every ounce of fruit is owing totally to the sovereign power of God. What other reason do we have to pray for the lost? If God is not the one who can raise the dead and bring life to the soul, we may as well stand in the local graveyard and call for the bodies to rise. This is why we pray. J. I. Packer has said it well:

> "You pray for the conversion of others. In what terms, now, do you intercede for them? Do you limit yourself to asking that God will bring them to a point where they can save themselves, independently of Him? I do not think you do. I think that what you do is to pray in categorical terms that God will, quite simply and decisively, save them: that He will open the eyes of their understanding, soften their hard hearts, renew their natures, and move their wills to receive the Saviour. You ask God to work in them everything necessary for their salvation. You would not dream of making it a point in your prayer that you are not asking God actually to bring them to faith, because you recognize that this is something He cannot do. Nothing of the sort! When you pray for unconverted people, you do so on the as-

sumption that it is in God's power to bring them to faith. You entreat Him to do that very thing, and your confidence in asking rests upon the certainty that He is able to do what you ask. And so indeed He is: that conviction, which animates your intercessions, is God's own truth, written on your heart by the Holy Spirit. In prayer, then (and the Christian is at his sanest and wisest when he prays), you *know* that it is God who saves men; you *know* that what makes men turn to God is God's own gracious work of drawing them to Himself; and the content of your prayers is determined by this knowledge. Thus, by your practice of intercession, no less than by giving thanks for your conversion, you acknowledge and confess the sovereignty of God's grace. And so do all Christian people everywhere." [85]

This understanding of God's work in the heart is the greatest motivation for a life of prayer. If we believe our real target is man's will–to secure a consent, an agreement, a decision–we will pray less and invent all manner of appealing, persuasive arts and techniques to get man to make *his* all-important decision. We will spend our time planning extravagant programs, developing professional presentations of music, and dressing up the gospel sales pitch with endless promises of "what it can do for you."

The simple, yet laborious ministry of prayer–burdened intercession– is laid aside while we plan and do the things that will "attract" sinners and "persuade" them to believe. Is it any wonder our churches are full of people who do not pray, witness, and study the Word? Is it any wonder that the Law of God seems archaic, dull, and restrictive to twentieth-century churchmen? Is it any wonder that stewardship campaigns, revivals, and

# ELECTION AND PRAYER

Sunday School contests are necessary to keep interest afloat? We have forsaken the secret place of prayer because our watered-down theology has bidden us to take matters into our own hands and not depend upon the Spirit of God alone to anoint the preaching of the gospel. God alone can change the heart through the foolishness of preaching–not our programs, organization, persuasive art, campaigns, or smooth counseling techniques. So, brethren, let us put away all our psychology, flash, and big plans to program and produce our calculated results and humbly wait upon our sovereign God in prayer.

If today's churches are not careful, the efforts that we do make in prayer might also be questioned. With much emphasis on awards, contests, recognition, advancing in the per-capita lists, moving up the denominational ladder and the resulting competition between churches and pastors, there is a very subtle, yet cancerous danger lying in wait. Are we really burdened for God's Name to be vindicated and His righteousness spread? Or do we pray for conversions because we desire more members for our clubs (churches). More souls mean better offerings and better offerings mean bigger buildings and more influence in the denomination. If we are not careful, the trap of trying to win Cooperative Program awards or to have our church's name announced at the next meeting could become the bottom-line concern for evangelism and motivator for prayer.

We are to pray out of hearts longing to see the glory of God revealed and His name vindicated in a blaspheming world. God's people cry out for the day when God's righteousness will cover the earth and His will is done exclusively in the earth as it is in heaven. His righteousness is our soul's delight. His glory is our crown of rejoicing. We grieve to see His truth being disregarded and His Name slandered in this earth. We plead,

# UNCONDITIONAL ELECTION

"Lord, reveal Your glory, extend Your arm, unsheath Your sword, make known Your righteousness." We labor incessantly to bring sinners to God as trophies of His grace that all the earth, with the heavenly hosts, might be shown the exceeding riches of our God's grace and fall in endless praise for the glory of His grace (Ephesians 1:6; 2:7).

This is why we pray. We love our God and we are jealous for His praise. We need no earthly awards to motivate us. We plead with God for men as we plead with men for God, not only with urgent concern for men's salvation, but also with an agonizing concern for the glorious honor of God.

## HUMILITY

Human pride fights and scratches for every grain of dignity it can possibly salvage for itself. Human pride is the chief voice to object to Unconditional Election. It is for this reason that Paul answers, "But indeed, O man, who are you to reply against God?" (Romans 9:20) The root problem is pride. Man likes to think of himself more highly than he ought to think, and the doctrine of election brings him down to nothingness– nothing to boast of, nothing to cling to, nothing to hold up, nothing to offer, nothing to claim, nothing to contribute. Unconditional Election destroys the last vestiges of human pride by laying the axe to the root of self. God's grace is glorified while the sinner's unworthiness and inability are magnified. When human beings apprehend God's sovereign majesty as Isaiah did (Isaiah 6), with a more realistic view of their own inward corruption and vileness, then they are abased and God is truly seen as GOD.

When men are humbled before a thrice-holy God who holds their eternal souls in His sovereign hands to do with as He pleases, mercy and grace take on new meaning. There is no bargaining for salvation's benefits. Repentance no longer appears as a strict duty or an unfair expectation, but rather as a privilege, a joy, and a hope for the soul. When God is properly seen by a sinner's eyes, he trembles. His soul melts, his ego is devastated. His opinion of self is blown to bits. He is awakened to his frightful plight as a stubborn rebel deserving of hell's deepest hole. He is made to fear God. This is why J. B. Gambrell suggested that by the preaching of those truths of God's sovereignty there would be "many slain of the Lord." The preaching of election "kills" pride. It goes right for the jugular; and is that not the way to the kingdom of God? Jesus said, "If any man desires to come after me, let him deny himself, and take up his cross daily, and follow Me. For whoever desires to save his life will lose it, but whoever loses his life for My sake will save it."

The preaching of the doctrines of sovereign grace is the appointed way of God to humble sinful hearts. Walt Chantry spoke to this point in his book, The Shadow of The Cross:

"True Calvinism always leads to the appreciation of self-denial. When the doctrines of grace are warmly and experimentally preached, denial of self is necessarily one of the chief experiences of the soul. Each one of the doctrines infinitely exalts the most high God and humbles the sinful and human self as a mere worm. What is it that you love about the doctrines of God's sovereignty and of human depravity? Is it not the wonder and realization of it all flooding your soul? Is

149

it not the blessed slaying of self-admiration, self-indulgence, self-satisfaction, self-determination . . . all of self?

"Is it not the rising beam of love to God with the prayer of Psalm ll5:1, 'Not unto us, O Lord, not unto us, but unto thy name give glory, for thy mercy, and for thy truth's sake'? Indeed it is the wrenching of our hearts from serving trite personal interests to glorifying God and enjoying Him for ever.

". . . One great benefit of the biblical truths called Calvinism is that they humble men in the dust. They make a man feel that 'the whole head is sick, and the whole heart faint. From the sole of the foot even unto the head there is no soundness in it; but wounds, and bruises, and putrifying sores' (Isaiah l:5-6). When this truth has seeped into the innermost man, he can no longer live for himself, but cries with Job, 'Wherefore I abhor *myself*, and repent in dust and ashes' (Job 42:6). Calvinism that does not humble has missed its mark." [86]

This humility of soul is carried through the conversion of a sinner as a foundation for his daily Christian walk. Those Christians who later come to understand doctrinally what they experienced inwardly also have a more Biblical foundation of humility to live their everyday lives. This foundation of humility before a sovereign Lord is that which will provide the Christian a more sensitive fear of God, a more willing submission to authorities and affliction, and a more gentle, forgiving spirit with the brethren. The Christian will still fight bloody battles with inward pride, but the foundational conviction of thorough humility is always there. A believer in sovereign grace has the heart perspective that is most likely not to resent God for afflictions sent or to magnify the faults of the brethren with self-righteous disdain. He will not sit back and refuse to serve the King of Glory whose mercy was so richly given. The thoroughly-humbled believer is extremely happy to be even the ear or the foot of the Body. It doesn't really matter if he is only the doorkeeper in the house of God. He is simply amazed and thrilled to have any part in the kingdom at all.

> While all our hearts and all our songs
>     Join to admire the feast,
> Each of us cries with thankful tongues,
>     "Lord, why was I a guest?"
>
> "Why was I made to hear thy voice,
>     And enter while there's room,
> When thousands make a wretched choice,
>     And rather starve than come?"
>
> 'Twas the same love that spread the feast
>     That sweetly drew us in;
> Else we had still refused to taste,
>     And perished in our sin.

Spiritual pride is always a threat to the Body of Christ. It was in Paul's day, and he had to remind the church at Corinth of their sovereign grace beginnings. He said, "None of you may be puffed up . . . *for who makes you to differ from another? And what do you have that you did not receive (I Corinthians 4:6,7)?*" The Apostle again referred the church back to its place of humility before the sovereign Bestower of all grace.

Much of the haughtiness, willfulness, and disputings in

# UNCONDITIONAL ELECTION

churches today would be greatly reduced if our people were humbled before a sovereign God of majesty. If professing Christians were trembling before the living God (Hebrews 10:31), the churches would be a greater storehouse of love and mutual respect. If professing Christians properly feared God and worked their jobs with a conscious awareness that the eye of the eternal God is upon them (Ephesians 6:5-9; Colossians 3:22-25), fewer worldlings would have cause to blaspheme.

We long to see more humbling, adoring evidences of saving gratitude displayed among God's people such as was demonstrated by the woman who poured out the costly ointment and wiped Jesus' feet with her hair (Luke 7:36-50). Jesus said the key to such loving adoration and humble sacrifice was a felt sense of personal forgiveness. Was this woman's self-effacing love poured out because of few sins forgiven or many? Jesus taught that the person who loves much will be the person who feels the greatness, the weightiness of his sin and guilt *removed*. That person will love Christ and serve God the most.

The doctrine of Unconditional Election elevates God's sovereign holiness and justice, magnifies the wickedness of man's heart, and glories in the free grace and mercy of God through Christ. Unconditional Election makes the distance between God and sinners far greater than any human opinions are willing to allow. This is why the Baptist Faith and Message says the doctrine of election "excludes boasting and promotes humility." It also creates in men's hearts a greater gratitude and wonder for mercy and grace in the forgiveness of sins. Unconditional Election, when burned into the soul of a man by the Holy Spirit, will make men more grateful and more devoted in their worship and service, as well as more loving and forgiving to their brethren in Christ.

# ELECTION AND GOOD WORKS

## GOOD WORKS

The good works of the Christian life were ordained of God at the same time our election took place (Ephesians 2:10). They were carefully prepared and designed for God's chosen people before the world began. These good works make God's elect "look" like God's people. When God chose us "in Him before the foundation of the world" (Ephesians 1:4), the "good works" of the Christian Life were automatically involved.

They are the "good works" of Jesus Christ. His character, His life, His attitudes–everything was settled–our lifestyles were ordained by God to be reflections of the One in whom our election was placed. They show His Son–His likeness–His image (Romans 8:29). When God's people live a life of conformity to God's Son they are revealing a sovereign and holy God in the midst of a dark world. There can be no divorcing the "high doctrine" of election from living the daily Christian life.

The very purpose of election in the mind of God, on the human side of things, was to raise up a "chosen generation, a royal priesthood, a holy nation, a peculiar people (special treasure)." This people would be a proclamation of God's praises–of the One who sovereignly called them out of darkness into His marvelous light (I Peter 2:9). The Almighty chose, elected, and predestinated us to be His children, that we should be holy and without blame before Him (Ephesians 1:4-5).

No one has any Biblical right to lay claim to be God's elect or His child if holiness of daily life is not top priority. "Without *holiness* no man shall see the Lord" (Hebrews 12:14). "But we are bound to give thanks to God always for you, brethren beloved by the Lord, because God from the beginning chose you for salvation through *sanctification* by the Spirit and belief in the truth" (II Thessalonians 2:13). God has elected and is saving a people to be a holy people. They are not a perfect people and they are not a spotless people, but on the whole of their lives, they are a holy people. They are different—distinct—a people who fear God and keep His commandments. They have been changed supernaturally with a righteous seed planted in the garden of their hearts and, notwithstanding their daily battles with remaining sin, their heartbeat is delight in God's Law and eagerness for God's glory. God's commandments are not grievous to them. To the contrary—they "delight to do thy will, O God." Their meat is to do the will of Him who called and sent them. There is no cost too great—no sacrifice too unreasonable —no service or labors above and beyond the call of duty.

The woman of Luke 7:36-50 poured out a sacrificial gift of great expense without concern for its great cost. Notice it was not to make the church building prettier or to get the church's name higher up the list in per-capita giving charts. She didn't have to sit through a special program to promote stewardship. She could not be stopped from sacrificially giving. No begging. No pleading. No sales pitch to coerce her to "support" the Savior. She gave purely out of love for Christ. Isaiah showed the same self-abandoning service to God (Isaiah 6). Why? Because He had seen God. God's glorious and sovereign majesty brought the prophet to vile nothingness. Preaching God's sovereignty in election does not breed sloth and unconcern! Sovereign mercy makes a man quickly respond with a "Here am I! Send me." Walt Chantry points out the impact of Calvinism on living the Christian life:

# ELECTION AND GOOD WORKS

"The doctrines of grace are not merely a philosophy which gives the best and most logical answers to the profound questions of life. They are that. But more, they stir the inner man to self-abnegation and love for Jehovah. This act of worship before the throne of the Almighty opens a fountain of devotion which must then flow out at every level of decision and action in the practical life. Self-denial is a vital link between doctrine and devotion on the one hand and between devotion and practice on the other. The author of amazing grace leads to the devotional act of self-denial, which in turn must demonstrate itself in daily living. The true test of your Calvinism comes just here. How low is self and how high is God in your heart? Almost every moment of your life offers a test.

The logical conclusion, the practical application of every element of God's sovereign grace, is found in the expression of 2 Corinthians 5:15, 'He died for all, that they which live should not henceforth live unto themselves, but unto him which died for them and rose again.' This was Paul's grand explanation of the Christian life." [87]

The apostles reminded their readers of the foundational reason as to why Christians are to spend their lives working for God. *In view of God's mercies* (Romans 12:1), Paul said, reflecting upon *God's electing mercy* from Romans 8-11, "you should give your bodies and minds (12:1,2) to serve God in the church (12:3-8), in loving brethren and enemies (12:9-21), in obeying the government (13:1-7), in living a life of godly love (13:8-14), and in practicing self-denying Christian liberty (Chapters 14, 15)." What the Holy Spirit is really saying through the

# UNCONDITIONAL ELECTION

Apostle Paul is this—You must understand God's electing purpose and electing mercies before you will be able to live the daily Christian life of holiness and good works in the way our God desires. Every action and reaction in the Christian's life is to flow from a sanctified heart and mind that has been shaped by the grace of Unconditional Election.

In Colossians 3:12 Paul established the reminder that they were God's elect before going on to teach them how to keep their hearts and their interpersonal relationships in the home and on the job. In I Peter 2, Peter uses election as the launching pad (1:2; 2:9,10) to explore the duties of submission in the believer's daily life for the rest of the book of I Peter. These passages make evident the fact that until the truth of election has been grasped to some degree, the believer will not be able to comprehend fully the Biblical perspective on his daily duties and service to God in a life of good works.

It is also this "high doctrine" that moves the hearts of God's elect to bring their daily burdens to God in prayer—Luke 18:7. With a sense of such a secure and intimate relationship with their God, *His elect* are encouraged to apply to the throne of grace for their Father's mercy. There is great significance in Jesus' identifying the widow and all those like her as God's <u>elect</u>. No other description of God's people would do. Jesus did not refer to His people here as His children, sons, or sheep, which terms might convey a gracious reception and intimate relationship. Jesus taught that ultimately the *very opposite* relationship from a helpless, abandoned, afflicted widow who petitions an unjust and heartless judge is to be found in *God's elect* coming to their sovereign Lord who lovingly invites their persistent prayers and will speedily care for their needs.

When your heart is grieved, when you are oppressed with

affliction, when clouds of despair overshadow your soul–understand this, dear child of God–the very God who has loved you ere the world began and who has cradled your soul in His omnipotent arms long before you knew Him, tenderly invites you to draw near to His throne of grace as His redeemed elect. All the rest, comfort, and soul assurance we need, as well as sovereign intervention in the affairs of our lives, are to be obtained from our God who encourages us to approach Him upon the basis of our election.

How sad that many who refuse to embrace the truths of electing grace will never understand the depth of God's love and will never appreciate the intimacy of union with Christ to be known only through sovereign grace. What peace! What assurance! What joy! To live every day serving our God, confident that no one dare bring a charge against God's elect (Romans 8:33), for it is God who justifies and it is Christ who intercedes as our attorney (Romans 8:34). His electing, conquering love holds us and forever, until we are glorified (Romans 8:30), keeps us in union with Christ working in us both to will and to do of His good pleasure (Philippians 2:13).

The daily assurance of God's persevering love cannot possibly be felt in the soul of a saint in greatest measure without an apprehension of the sovereignty and eternality of God's love. It is this wondrous love in us that acts in us to produce good works in Jesus' Name that will turn the heads of the men in this earth to glorify our Father in heaven (Matthew 5:16).

Dear reader, do you see why the doctrine of election has everything to do with your daily walk? Do you realize how this sublime truth is not to be regarded as nonessential or sterile theology? It has everything to do with how a Christian will daily see himself, his world, his life and calling, and more importantly, his God.

# UNCONDITIONAL ELECTION

### *The Sovereignty of Grace*
*Luke 10:21-22*

1. *There was an hour when Christ rejoiced,*
   *And spoke his joy in words of praise:*
   *"Father, I thank thee, mighty God,*
   *"Lord of the earth, and heavens, and seas.*

2. *"I thank thy sovereign power and love,*
   *"That crowns my doctrine with success;*
   *"And makes the babes in knowledge learn*
   *"The heights, and breadths, and lengths of grace.*

3. *"But all this glory lies concealed*
   *"From men of prudence and of might;*
   *"The prince of darkness blinds their eyes,*
   *"And their own pride resists the light.*

4. *"Father, 'tis thus, because thy will*
   *"Chose and ordained it should be so;*
   *"Tis thy delight t' abase the proud,*
   *"And lay the haughty scorner low.*

5. *"There's none can know the Father right,*
   *"But those who learn it from the Son;*
   *"Nor can the Son be well received,*
   *"But where the Father makes him known."*

6. *Then let our souls adore our God,*
   *Who deals his graces as he please;*
   *Nor gives to mortals an account,*
   *Or of his actions, or decrees.*

*HYMN TUNES: Waltham, Maryton* [88]

# CONCLUSION

The heritage is glorious. The doctrinal foundation of the Southern Baptist Convention was clearly the truths delineated and emphasized in the Protestant Reformation–

"Sola Scriptura" - The Bible alone!

"Sola Gratia" - The Grace of God alone!

"Sola Fide" - By Faith alone!

"Sola Deo Gloria" - For God's Glory alone!

These truths say it all. Man is not to look to church or denomination dogma. He is not to look to any act, work, obedience, or cooperation he can perform. He is not to have any confidence whatsoever in his own abilities or attractiveness. He is not to entertain any motives of self interest or self glory. The essence of Biblical Christianity funnels back every time to this conclusion–the higher God is seen to be, and the lower man is seen to be, the better. Put a knife to the throat of humanism–secular or Christian. God will share His glory with none. For the blood-bought child of God, the "joy unspeakable and full of glory" is in gazing steadfastly upon the Lover of his soul, who by sovereign grace, has dispensed saving mercy and caused him to have inward delight for the exaltation of God alone. The Word of God, the Grace of God, and the Glory of God are all that really matter in this life.

The road to earthly popularity is not marked by these signs of God-centeredness. The natural man will not gravitate with hopeful anticipation to sit under the declaration of such truths. There are more effective ways to keep the baptismal waters splashing and the membership rolls expanding. There is a price to be paid by the person who speaks with solemnity of the awful implications of God's sovereign holiness. God's love and grace will not be recognizable anymore to the churchman who is trotting selfishly through life with no apparent fear of God. The careful minister of the Gospel will be accused of making the Gospel too complicated, too demanding, and too harsh. He will exchange denominational clout for the stigma of being an independent thinker–a rabble rouser of sorts. Try as he may to blend in with the mainstream of cooperative institutionalism, he will find that to preach the old truths of the Founders will mean a whole new set of problems for his ministry. Even that in itself should tell us something.

This presentation of the doctrine of Unconditional Election has no political agenda within the Southern Baptist Convention. If Southern Baptists were believing and preaching the faith of our founders, there would be no political camps or campaigning as we see today. Our energies spent to secure great numbers of voting delegates would be rather channeled into world missions. How sad that such confusion and strife has crowded out our faithful obedience to the Great Commission.

The Word of God is still calling men to boldly declare the glories of Jehovah. In our man-centered, humanistic age, courage is indispensable. To look modern man in the eye and speak of a Christ-exalting Gospel, without seeking to entice or smooth it over with appealing goodies, indeed requires courage. To preach real repentance, total depravity, absolute sovereignty, human bondage to sin, God's conquering grace, and the final authority of God's Word, necessitates courage. But a man, called of God, whose heart is aflame with the Word of God, cannot keep the truth shut up in his bones for long. The Spirit of the Lord will make his voice a trumpet of Divine truth. The Spirit of the Lord will lift up the messenger's soul with inward conviction to face the most violent and the most smug of the twentieth century. Standing alone, facing rejection, even being made the offscouring of all things, is cause for rejoicing, since these things accentuate our reward in heaven and place us in the esteemed company of the persecuted prophets (Matthew 5:12). If you are seeking to be faithful to the Scriptures in your life and ministry, let this encouragement fill your soul and strengthen your hands.

Dear friend, make a careful study of the doctrine of Unconditional Election. Search the Scriptures objectively with this truth in mind. You will begin to see God's sovereign grace everywhere in the Word of God. You will be surprised to see how much of the Bible you have never seen before. It has happened with so many people, and it is happening today on a grand scale. Many Southern Baptists are coming back to the "Old Paths." Our greatest concern is to get folks wrestling with the foundational truth of Election and to see it once again understood and preached as it was in days gone by. If the Founders saw it as the heart and hub of all Bible truth, brethren, there must be something to it. As we saw in Chapter four, this truth forms and shapes all the practical expressions of our Christian faith. It will make a difference.

There are several misconceptions about Unconditional Election that I would like to address again before I close. First, God does not save or damn anyone against his will. At no point have I suggested that God disregards the human will. Unconditional Election is God's saving purpose which works compatibly with and not contrary to the human will. For those who will be damned, God leaves them to and gives them exactly what they choose for themselves. For those who are going to be saved, God sovereignly and graciously changes their hearts through the

# UNCONDITIONAL ELECTION

Holy Spirit and the Gospel so that they voluntarily and eagerly trust the Lord Jesus for salvation by their own choice. Without God's sovereign, quickening power, none would respond and be saved.

Secondly, anyone who is saved must hear the Gospel and believe. This is the way God has ordained to bring in His elect. There is no other way. We must preach. We must witness. We must seek to bring people to hear the truths of saving grace. Christ, the Lord of the Church, has commissioned us to this task. We must give ourselves tirelessly, yea, relentlessly, to this duty of the Great Commission until all the strangers are brought home.

Thirdly, the Gospel is to be preached to *every* creature on this earth. There is to be no discrimination of any kind. Our God is worthy to be made known to the far corners of the earth, and He will powerfully save sinners from every nook and cranny of the entire globe. Christ died to save men of all kinds out of every tribe and tongue and people and nation. Our call is to beseech men everywhere, without distinction, to repent.

Fourthly, God receives every single person who comes to Him in faith through Jesus Christ. All who come to Him will in no way be cast out. If anyone comes to Him on real and true Gospel terms, they will experience the open embrace and saving mercies of King Jesus. Come one and all—come according to Christ's Gospel and find salvation.

I feel the need to underscore these points in order to alleviate suspicions that Unconditional Election belongs only to Primitive Baptists or to other "hyper-Calvinists". To the contrary—serious Calvinists through the centuries have been warm and experimental in their practice of godliness and world-wide evangelism. They have prayed for the revival of God's

162

# CONCLUSION

glorious grace to be felt powerfully at home and abroad through missions. Any man who does not burn with passion to see sinners converted is no true Calvinist.

This was the doctrinal foundation of the Southern Baptist Convention. History does not change. The facts are there. Absolute Predestination and Unconditional Election are compatible with evangelism and missions. Our forefathers proved that. These historic truths of sovereign grace freely directed the worship, church life, Sunday Schools, seminaries, mission boards, publications, convention meetings, and hymn books. The pulpits fearlessly announced a sovereign God who freely disposes of His saving mercies according to His own good pleasure. The need today is to return to the "Old Paths". The Christian faith today again needs to brandish the sword of the Spirit with the sharpest cutting edge possible as the battle grows more intense. Only the fulness of God's saving truth is able to withstand the onslaughts of a hellish enemy and give the Church of Christ a penetrating, conquering militancy that will gain the victory. The need today can be summed up best, and I can put it in no better words than to again hear the twentieth-century call of Brother J. B. Gambrell saying:

> "We may invigorate our faith and renew our courage by reflecting that divine power has always attended the preaching of doctrine when done in the true spirit of preaching. Great revivals have accompanied the heroic preaching of the doctrines of grace–predestination, election, and that whole lofty mountain range of doctrines upon which Jehovah sits enthroned, sovereign in grace, as in all things else. God honors the preaching that honors Him. There is entirely too much milk-sop preaching nowadays–trying to cajole sinners to enter

163

upon a truce with their Maker—'Quit sinning and join the church.' The situation does not call for a truce, but for a surrender. Let us bring on the heavy artillery of heaven and thunder away at the stuck-up age as Whitefield, Edwards, Spurgeon, and Paul did and there will be many slain of the Lord raised up to walk in newness of life."

May our God be pleased to rebuild the foundations and to exalt His Son for the glory of His Name, until His righteousness and majesty cover the earth!

# BIBLIOGRAPHY

1. Dr. Thomas J. Nettles. By His Grace and For His Glory , (Grand Rapids Baker Book House Co., 1986), p. 216. Used by permission.
2. James P. Boyce. Abstract of Systematic Theology, (Pompano Beach, Florida: Reprinted by the Christian Gospel Foundation, original copyright - 1887), p. 347, 348.
3. Ibid., The Abstract of Principles are found on the last page of this reprinted edition.
4. Ibid., also last page.
5. Dr. Thomas J. Nettles. Lecture given at the 1982 Council on Baptist Theology entitled, "Baptists and the Doctrines of Grace".
6. Nettles. By His Grace and For His Glory, pp. 381, 382.
7. Edwin S. Gaustad. Baptist Piety: The Last Will and Testimony of Obadiah Holmes, (Grand Rapids: W. B. Eerdmans Pub. Co., 1978), pp. 83, 84. Used by permission.
8. Nettles. By His Grace and For His Glory, p. 62.
9. Kenneth H. Good. Are Baptists Calvinists?, (Oberlin, OH: Regular Baptist Heritage Fellowship, 1975), p. 167.
10. Matthew Henry. Matthew Henry's Commentary of the Whole Bible, Vol. 6, Acts - Revelation. (New Jersey: Fleming H. Revell Co.), pp. 423, 424, 446.
11. Jonathan Edwards. The Works of Jonathan Edwards, Vol. 1. (Edinburgh: Banner of Truth, 1976), pp. 84, 88.*
12. Arnold Dallimore. George Whitefield, Vol. 1 (Edinburgh: Banner of Truth, 1975), pp. 407, 408.*
13. Nettles. By His Grace and For His Glory, pp. 139, 136.

# BIBLIOGRAPHY

14. John Newton. The Works of the Rev. John Newton, (Edinburgh: Thomas Nelson, 1849), p. 55.
15. L. Russ Bush and Tom J. Nettles. Baptists and the Bible, (Chicago, Moody Press, 1980), pp. 112, 113. Used by permission.
16. Kenneth H. Good. Are Baptists Calvinists?, p. 169.
17. Iain Murray. The Puritan Hope, (Edinburgh: Banner of Truth, 1971), p. 145.*
18. Nettles. Lecture. (see footnote #1).
19. Nettles. By His Grace and For His Glory, p. 153.
20. Bush and Nettles. Baptists and the Bible, pp. 149, 150.
21. Nettles. By His Grace and For His Glory, p.157.
22. Dr. Thomas J. Nettles. Southern Baptist Sermons on Sovereignty and Responsibility, (Harrisonburg, VA: Sprinkle Pub., 1984), pp 1-22.
23. Dr. Thomas J. Nettles. Article written in the CBC Report of Continental Baptist Churches, (Wheaton, IL: Continental Baptist Churches, Feb. 1984).
24. The Baptist Confession of Faith of 1689, (Sterling, VA: Grace Abounding Ministries), pp. 12, 13, 22, 23.
25. Nettles. Southern Baptist Sermons, pp. 34-61.
26. Nettles. CBC Report, Feb. 1984.
27. Nettles. Southern Baptist Sermons, p. 65, 66.
28. Nettles. By His Grace and For His Glory, pp. 164, 165.
29. Nettles. CBC Report, Feb. 1984.
30. Nettles. Southern Baptist Sermons, pp. 111, 112, 115.
31. John Broadus. Memoirs of J. P. Boyce, (New York, A. C. Armstrong and Son, 1893), pp. 112, 113.
32. Dr. Paige Patterson. Dr. Patterson wrote a recommendation for the book Manual of Theology and Church Order by J. L. Dagg. The recommendation is found on the

# BIBLIOGRAPHY

cover flap.

33. J. L. Dagg. <u>Manual of Theology and Church Order,</u> (Harrisonburg, VA: Sprinkle Pub., 1982), pp. 305-313.

34. Bush and Nettles. <u>Baptists and the Bible</u>, p. 162.

35. Patrick Hues Mell. <u>A Southern Baptist Looks at Predestination,</u> Ft. Worth, TX: Reprinted by The Wicket Gate, Grace Baptist Fellowship), pp. 31, 32.

36. Dr. Thomas J. Nettles. The biographical sketch of P. H. Mell, found on pp. 7, 8 of Mell's book, <u>A Southern Baptist Looks at Predestination</u>.

37. Boyce. <u>Abstract of Systematic Theology</u>, pp. 347, 348.

38. Broadus. <u>Memoirs of J. P. Boyce,</u> p. 265.

39. Ibid., p. 266.

40. Dr. Thomas J. Nettles, editor. <u>Baptist Catechisms,</u> (Memphis, TN: Mid-America Baptist Seminary), p. 227.

41. Ibid., pp. 236, 237.

42. Elgin S. Moyer. <u>Who Was Who in Church History,</u> (New Canaan, CT: Keats Pub. Co., 1974), p. 59.

43. Ernest C. Reisinger. From the Publisher's Introduction to J.P. Boyce's <u>Abstract of Systematic Theology</u>, p. XVI.

44. Broadus. <u>Memoirs of J. P. Boyce</u>, pp. 308-310.

45. Nettles. <u>Baptist Catechisms</u>, p. 248.

46. Moyer. <u>Who Was Who in Church History</u>, p. 385.

47. Reisinger. Publisher's Introduction. <u>Abstract</u>, p. XXI.

48. C. H. Spurgeon. <u>Spurgeon on the Five Points,</u> (Florida: Tyndale Bible Society), p. 67.

49. Nettles. Lecture, (See footnote #1).

50. Bush and Nettles. <u>Baptists and the Bible</u>, p. 246.

51. Arthur Custance. <u>The Sovereignty of Grace,</u> (Phillipsburg, N. J.: Pres. and Reformed Pub. Co., 1979), pp. 135, 136.

52. Spurgeon. <u>Spurgeon on the Five Points</u>, p. 98.

# BIBLIOGRAPHY

53. Erroll Hulse. <u>An Introduction To The Baptists,</u> (Sussex, England: Carey Pub., 1973), p. 92.
54. B. H. Carroll. <u>Commentary on Acts,</u> pp. 279, 280.
55. Nettles. Lecture, (See footnote #1).
56  Arthur Custance. <u>The Sovereignty of Grace</u>, pp. 135, 136.
57. Broadus. <u>Memoirs of J. P. Boyce</u>, pp. 153, 154, 169. Williams also helped to draw up the Abstract of Principles and signed it as a professor at Southern Seminary.
58. Abstract of Principles. <u>Abstract of Systematic Theology</u>, last page.
59. Nettles. Lecture, (See footnote #1).
60. Nettles. <u>By His Grace and For His Glory</u>, pp. 212, 213.
61. Ibid., pp. 217, 218.
62. Ibid., pp. 219, 220.
63. Ibid., p. 207.
64. Nettles. Lecture, (See footnote #1).
65. Nettles. <u>By His Grace and For His Glory</u>, p. 217.
66. Ibid., p. 217.
67. W. T. Connor. <u>Christian Doctrine</u>, (Nashville, TN: Broadman Press, 1937), pp. 155-158.
68. Nettles. <u>By His Grace</u>, pp. 267, 283, 425, 426.
69. Iain Murray. <u>The Forgotten Spurgeon</u>, (Edinburgh: Banner of Truth, 1978), pp. 100, 101.*
70. C. Samuel Storms. <u>Chosen For Life,</u> (Grand Rapids: Baker Book House Co., 1987), p. 84. Used by permission.
71. R. C. Sproul. <u>Chosen By God,</u> (Wheaton: Tyndale House Pub., Inc., 1986), pp. 69, 70. Used by permission.
72. Boyce. <u>Abstract of Systematic Theology</u>, pp. 388, 389.
73. Tom Wells. <u>Faith: The Gift of God,</u> (Edinburgh: Banner of Truth, 1983), Chapter 9.*
74. C. H. Spurgeon. A sermon entitled <u>Election</u>, reprinted by

# BIBLIOGRAPHY

Chapel Library, Venice, FL, p.15.

75. Murray. The Forgotten Spurgeon, p. 56.*
76. Ibid., pp 72, 73.*
77. J. I. Packer. Evangelism and the Sovereignty of God, (Downers Grove, IL: Intervarsity Press, 1961), pp. 27-29. Used by permission.
78. Iain Murray. D. Martyn Lloyd-Jones, The First Forty Years, (Edinburgh: Banner of Truth, 1982), p. 207.*
79. Ernest C. Reisinger. Today's Evangelism, (Phillipsburg: Craig Press, 1982), p. 108.
80. Joseph Tracy. The Great Awakening, (Edinburgh: Banner of Truth, 1976, first published in 1842), pp. 10, 11.*
81. Bennet Tyler and Andrew Bonar. The Life and Labours of Asahel Nettleton, (Edinburgh: Banner of Truth) pp. 310, 311, 376, 377, 282, 289, 242, 243, 120, 404, 405, 244, 245.*
82. Reisinger. Today's Evangelism, pp. 74-76.
83. Iain Murray. The Invitation System, (Edinburgh: Banner of Truth, 1973), pp. 36-38. *
84. Murray. The Forgotten Spurgeon, pp. 113, 114.*
85. Packer. Evangelism and the Sovereignty of God, pp. 15, 16.
86. Walter J. Chantry. The Shadow of the Cross, (Edinburgh: Banner of Truth, 1981), pp. 8, 9.*
87. Ibid., p. 10.
88. These Hymn Selections are taken from the Conference Hymn Book of the Southern Baptist Founders Conference. Originally, these hymns were selected by a committee who were requested by the Board of Directors of the American Baptist Publication and Sunday School Society to suggest acceptable hymns to the churches. Among those on the committee were J. L. Dagg, R. B. C. Howell, and William Williams.

* All Banner of Truth quotes used by permission.